HOW THE FORCE
CAN FIX THE WORLD

HOW THE FORCE
CAN FIX THE WORLD

LESSONS ON LIFE, LIBERTY, AND HAPPINESS
FROM A GALAXY FAR, FAR AWAY

STEPHEN KENT

CENTER
STREET

New York • Nashville

Center Street
Hachette Book Group
1290 Avenue of the Americas, New York, NY 10104
centerstreet.com
twitter.com/centerstreet

First Edition: October 2021

Center Street is a division of Hachette Book Group, Inc. The Center Street name and logo are trademarks of Hachette Book Group, Inc.

The publisher is not responsible for websites (or their content) that are not owned by the publisher.

The Hachette Speakers Bureau provides a wide range of authors for speaking events. To find out more, go to www.HachetteSpeakersBureau.com or call (866) 376-6591.

Illustrations by Aaron Gray / Illustrations © 2021 by Stephen Kent

Library of Congress Control Number: 2021942533

ISBNs: 978-1-5460-0046-4 (hardcover), 978-1-5460-0048-8 (ebook)

Printed in the United States of America

LSC-C

Printing 1, 2021

For Sylvie.

If Star Wars can't help heal this broken world,

I have no doubt that you can.

The Force will be with you, always.

And so will I.

CONTENTS

FOREWORD: PART I

by Ben Domenech
Publisher of *The Federalist* & Fox News contributor

O F THE MANY REGRETS I have in life, few rival the time I commanded that Wookiee to kill the poor Twi'lek girl on the sunny shores of Lehon.

That scene, an infamous ethical decision within the 2003 *Star Wars: Knights of the Old Republic* video game, still haunts many a player who chose the path of the dark side, wanting to unlock the fearsome Force lightning ability without incurring any cost. The moment indicates the depth of archetype and myth contained within the Star Wars universe, inspiring emotion with utterly unfamiliar characters who still manage to make you feel the disturbance of their deaths.

We've all heard the critique of Star Wars fandom that comes primarily from those who support "hard sci-fi"—though that seems rather laughable when it refers to the broad range of works from Isaac Asimov, Robert Heinlein, Liu Cixin, Neal Stephenson, or Arthur C. Clarke.

Why is someone who dreams of epic stories that span the space between the stars compelled to choose between *The Expanse* and *Dune*, *Blade Runner* or *Ghost in the Shell*, Star Wars or Star Trek?

It's possible to love the Beatles and the Rolling Stones, you know. You can even love Elvis and the Beach Boys, but not to the same degree.

I grew up devouring the hard sci-fi books and short stories of these authors. Like well-written comic books, they were fantastical and still surprisingly in touch with the deep emotional and ethical nature of humanity. You learned about friendship and honor from Han Solo and Captain America alike.

But no universe approaches the kind of depth that Star Wars continually reaches. Dismiss it if you wish. Deride it all as savvy toy marketing to kids or tireless service to fanboys with easter eggs disguised as a plot. In a free society you're free to be wrong. Star Wars is the closest thing we have to modern Arthurian legend.

Knights, wizards, and princesses (who are most assuredly not damsels in distress) confronting the monsters of a long time ago in a galaxy far, far away, speak to the deepest heroic ambitions within all of us. Leia slaying Jabba is as iconic as Perseus offing Medusa; Anakin and Obi-Wan's face-off surrounded by the flames of Mustafar is as intense as Achilles's duel with Hector; and then there is the metal-clad Din Djarin, the Mandalorian, who overcomes a Krayt dragon on the desolate world of Tatooine.

"Fairy tales do not give the child his first idea of bogey," G. K. Chesterton wrote. "What fairy tales give the child is his first clear idea of the possible defeat of bogey. The baby has known the dragon intimately ever since he had an imagination. What the fairy tale provides for him is a St. George to kill the dragon."

Star Wars has far more to offer us than logic puzzles and the increasingly woke world of comic books, fantasy, and science fiction. The Skywalker family drama is Shakespearean in its stakes, roiling at the center of a maelstrom of galactic conflict which has surged before and will arise again. The series compels us to weigh the arguments of all sides. The way of the Sith may seem on its face like a religious excuse for an evil fascistic regime— but what if it cares more about the direction of the galaxy, on preventing chaos and providing order, than the uncaring, naive, and often aloof Jedi?

One of the best minor characters in Jon Favreau's Mandalorian series on Disney+ is Mayfeld, depicted by GOAT Boston comedian Bill Burr. Mayfeld is a jaded mercenary who views the work of the Rebellion and the Empire alike as nothing but a power play that is destructive to the invisible masses who are caught in the crossfire. His sarcasm turns serious, though, when confronted with a reminder of the evils in which he was complicit during his past as an Imperial soldier. Mayfeld is presented with a dangerous choice. Rather than shirk it for fear of the fray, he chooses a side.

Star Wars speaks to us as a timeless representation of human nature at war with its worst impulses. This is why it has something to say to us today. The very title is a lie. The war was never about the divide between the stars. As Aleksandr Solzhenitsyn wrote in *The Gulag Archipelago*, "The line separating good and evil passes not through states, nor between classes, nor between political parties either—but right through every human heart."

There is still some good in you. I can sense it. Even among those of us who made that Wookiee kill that Twi'lek. "Diogenes looked for his honest man inside every crypt and cavern," Chesterton wrote, "but he never thought of looking inside the thief." This means there is hope, even for the most broken of us, even in the dead-end isolation of a desert under twin suns.

May the Force be with you.

FOREWORD: PART II

by Betsy Hodges

47th mayor of Minneapolis

I WAS SEVEN YEARS OLD when my dad took my older brothers and me to see an unusual space movie. I remember not understanding what was happening, I remember being scared of Darth Vader, I remember being intrigued by Princess Leia, and most of all, I most indelibly remember the holographic chess set and the band in the cantina at Mos Eisley. We saw Star Wars, and life would never be the same.

But for me, Star Wars was more than just a story. It was a lifeline. Not long after I was introduced to that galaxy far, far away, I began to be sexually abused by people outside of my family, a horror that continued for years. I didn't tell anyone about it until I got sober at age nineteen.

Through all the darkness, Star Wars was there. When I was ten years old, my father got the first VHS in the neighborhood and a bootleg video of Star Wars. The ability to watch what you wanted whenever you wanted was a brand-new concept for everyone. I remember marveling, "You mean, I can just...watch it? Whenever I want?"

Watch it, I did. Dozens of times—if not hundreds. It was my comfort. To this day when anyone, anywhere, mentions Tatooine I am brought back to that warm desert and an acute sense of safety. Mos Eisley may be a wretched hive of scum and villainy, but to me it will always feel like home.

I was fourteen years old when *Return of the Jedi* was released. By then, the abuse had slowed down and my disconnection from people had sped up. I was jaded and lost. But there was a movie theater I could walk to from my house, and I earned enough money from babysitting and other jobs to buy my own tickets.

Return of the Jedi drew me to the theater five times. I was so happy to be back on Tatooine, if only for a little while. But I remember how confused I was by the end of the movie, when Luke dropped his lightsaber instead of violently vanquishing Darth Vader.

I was compelled by this act of faith. It seemed a new template for adulthood, different and better than the ones I'd seen in my own world. The moment Luke's lightsaber clattered to the floor of Emperor Palpatine's throne room was the moment I started to see the world a bit differently.

What I saw was this: we believe in each other's humanity, no matter what. When we lose that belief, we lose our own humanity. Luke Skywalker's choice remains a revelation to me to this day. The dark side is alluring, and it is rife in our current times.

We all feel it: the pull to blame, to attack, to criticize and to ostracize is made all the more powerful by the easy access we have to technological engines that feed on fear, anger, and shame.

But there's a better way—the way of the Force—which calls us to see the essential humanity of other people even at their worst and to retain our integrity as we stand against darkness.

I know how hard this can be. I have suffered evil up close. I've looked it in the eye. Reflecting on those eyes today, I see human beings in so much pain and confusion that they could no longer see or recognize my essential humanity, which meant they could not access their own. *That* is the dark side. The day I fully understood that my perpetrators had done nothing to me that hadn't been done to them was the day I could fully answer the call to the Light. Their behavior was unacceptable and inhuman, and to stand against it is an act of love. But I do not need to forget their basic humanness to do so. In fact, remembering our shared humanity is the only way forward that doesn't lead to the dark side.

Our politics have taken a sharp detour around our shared humanity. There's division, unkindness, and profound confusion surrounding how we relate to one another, especially those with whom we disagree. We are frequently tempted to forget all the things we have in common with our neighbors in favor of the ways we differ.

We need a guide to lead us back to one another. And as Mr. Kent ably demonstrates in this book, Star Wars can be that guide.

INTRODUCTION

THERE'S BEEN AN AWAKENING. Have you felt it?" Since 2015, when Star Wars returned from a decade-long slumber following the conclusion of George Lucas's prequel trilogy, this line from the first teaser trailer for *Episode VII: The Force Awakens* has rattled around in my mind, mixed with excitement and dread. Star Wars means the world to me and my family. The story of Darth Vader, Luke Skywalker, Princess Leia, and an evil empire's rise and fall is so much more than a piece of escapist entertainment we mindlessly view to combat boredom.

Star Wars is a lifestyle.

Star Wars is a philosophy.

It is something that has given me community ever since I was a kid. Now it does the same thing for my own youngling. The Force is strong in our family.

Of course, we're far from alone. As of 2021, Star Wars sits atop the film franchise world, boasting $10 billion in box office revenue, second only to the Marvel Cinematic Universe—which, with twenty-three films since 2008, has managed to overtake Star Wars only by way of sheer volume. Star Wars, however, has remained in the public consciousness since 1977 with a more measured approach—and it is working.

Surveys aggregated by Statista in 2019 show that only 37 percent of Americans do *not* consider themselves to be Star Wars fans.* Go to any Walmart, Target, or small-town toy shop in the country, and you'll find something with Darth Vader's likeness plastered on it. You'd probably be more likely to connect with a random stranger on the street over Star Wars—whether it's about Vader's role as the chief villain of the franchise, Princess Leia's iconic bun hairdo, the Death Star, or the light and dark sides of the Force—than over basic American history.

Seriously! Would you bet $100 on your tax accountant's ability to pick Boba Fett out of a lineup, or to identify President Thomas Jefferson? What about $200 on your neighbor's ability to recite their own rights under the Bill of Rights within the US Constitution, versus naming all the members of the Skywalker family? The odds are better than 3,720 to 1 (the

---

* "Share of adults who are fans of Star Wars in the United States as of July 2019, by age," Statista, https://www.statista.com/statistics/725506/star-wars-favorability-age/.

approximate odds of Han Solo and the Millennium Falcon successfully navigating an asteroid field) that your neighbor might actually nail the recitation of their own civil rights—so it's not impossible—but I'd go with Star Wars trivia any day of the week.

Star Wars is a cultural commons. I've always known this from personal experience. I was in the tenth grade when *Episode III: Revenge of the Sith* (2005) hit theaters. I'll never forget starting lunch break on the front lawn of my high school and sitting down with my friends, who were already busily chatting about the rise of Palpatine and the Empire, wondering aloud if America was on the same path with the George W. Bush administration. Obviously, that didn't happen, but it was fun to talk about. It helped a bunch of kids growing up in a time of fear and war digest what was happening on the news and relate it back to something slightly less charged.

The fictional lessons of Star Wars can be readily translated into real life. Democracy is not guaranteed. Liberty dies with thunderous applause. Good intentions can still lead to disaster.

The enduring appeal of Star Wars crystallized even more for me when I moved to Washington, DC, for work and started taking note of the casual use of Star Wars references to explain politics. In the aftermath of a 2015 Republican presidential debate hosted by CNBC, in which Jeb Bush and his political mentee, Senator Marco Rubio, clashed on a stage in Boulder, Colorado, the pundit class immediately started chattering about how the apprentice had become the master. On CNN, I remember one of the talking heads snarking about how Marco Rubio was no longer a "Padawan learner" to Governor Bush.

That's when I decided to start a Star Wars and politics podcast and title it *Beltway Banthas*. The podcast has always been about celebrating how even in a town where everything is about conflict and tribalism, Star Wars still manages to present its fans with a shared language with which to have otherwise tough discussions. You can go on YouTube and find the 2007 History Channel documentary by Ken Burns, *Star Wars: The Legacy Revealed*, and hear from both Newt Gingrich and Nancy Pelosi, two House speakers on different sides of the aisle, outlining how Star Wars makes discussing morality and good versus evil with your opponents just a little bit easier. It was true then and remains true today.

I've sat down to talk about life, politics, and morality with all manner of people since *Beltway Banthas* launched. Conservative talk radio shock jocks, liberal congressmen, socialist activists, staunch free-market libertarian purists, and everything in between. With Star Wars as a shared love, it's amazing the kinds of conflict I've been able to circumvent in those discussions about the Force, Skywalkers, and the Empire, when just beneath the surface lie incredibly weighty subjects like terrorism, race, political violence, taxation, and the role of government. The kinds of political subjects we often feel are impossible to discuss with those unlike ourselves become easier to talk about with the galaxy far, far away helping to mediate the conversation.

Star Wars is a buffer. A cross-cultural translation app that takes the sting out of sharing your heart or deeply personal beliefs with people who may not agree with the way you live or see the world. We need as much of it as we can get—just look around you.

The world isn't gathering around campfires to sing "Kumbaya" and find common ground. No. When I said that there was a sense of dread to the line "There's been an awakening. Have you felt it?" what I meant was that I have felt something akin to a venomous bite. There's a poison running through the veins of political discourse around the world that is making it more bitter, polarized, and, in some cases, even violent. You've seen it.

Polarization in our politics is showing up everywhere. It's in our social media feeds as friends who once bonded over shared hobbies publicly snipe about political news and disown one another over petty disagreements. Family members have become estranged from one another over politics. Maybe it's the constant visibility of your parents' political views in the online world, or the legitimately polarizing effects of news and information being served up on TV news and online, but we've all seen people we love morph into somewhat unrecognizable digital shadows of themselves. And it makes us both sad and angry.

I've worked in Washington since around 2014 in the policy and advocacy space. The trends pulling us all apart have been happening in slow motion for decades, but the fracturing has gone into light speed since I first arrived in town. Partisan enmity is surging. Whereas "Democrat" or "Republican" were once somewhat benign signifiers of a few eclectic political opinions, or maybe indicative of your zip code and upbringing, these political affiliations have morphed into toxic superidentities. A Democrat is far more likely to be a minority, make less than $25,000 a year, and live in a major metropolitan area. They're more likely to get their entertainment via streaming services like Netflix or Hulu than to buy cable packages, and they might have never set foot in a church in their lives. It didn't always used to be this way. But over time, our consumer habits, political preferences, and demographic signifiers have gotten more neatly aligned. As this has happened, we've not only become more predictable, but we have also geographically sorted ourselves in order to be around other people who are just like us. This has made us all more extreme in our views.

Group polarization, as described by the scholar Cass Sunstein, works something like a gravitational field.* The most extreme individuals in any group act like a sun, and they draw in surrounding stars (or group members) steadily by opening up the boundaries of the debate. Over time, as the mass of the sun increases, its gravitational force also increases. Soon the entire solar system is defined by the pull of that giant gaseous star. "The law of group polarization," the term coined by Sunstein

---

* Cass R. Sunstein, "The Law of Group Polarization," The University of Chicago Law School, 1999, https://chicagounbound.uchicago.edu/law_and_economics/542/.

to characterize this pull, can help to explain everything from internet echo chambers to community politics and even how armed rebellion can break out in a country. Sunstein has in fact written on how this principle applies to the Rebel Alliance in Star Wars in his 2016 book, *The World according to Star Wars.*

If you've seen the corrosiveness of affective polarization in your own life, you're not alone. And we've now gone a step beyond polarization. A 2020 Georgetown University poll showed that a majority of Americans feel that we're slowly coming apart as a country. Furthermore, respondents indicated that America was 67 percent of the way toward a second civil war.* That's terrifying. Not just because we can see that political violence is rising sharply, but because stories like that of Star Wars show us how our fears can so often be willed into reality.

I don't feel like I have to sell you further on the idea that the world is a mess or that politics has gotten to be horribly ugly. Those things are self-evident. Still, what I worry about is the corrosive effect of that fear and hostility permeating our culture.

"What has that got to do with anything?" is how a young Anakin Skywalker responded to a similar worry about how he dealt with fear in *Episode I: The Phantom Menace* (1999). To which Jedi Master Yoda responded, "Everything! Fear is the

---

* Adam A. Raymond, "How Close Is the U.S. to Civil War? About Two-Thirds of the Way, Americans Say," *New York* (magazine), October 24, 2019, https://nymag.com /intelligencer/2019/10/americans-say-u-s-is-two-thirds-of-the-way-to-civil-war.html.

path to the dark side. Fear leads to anger. Anger leads to hate. Hate…leads to suffering."

This is the path we're on. Where do you think we are in the sequence?

Regardless, it's not too late to turn the tide against the forces of darkness clouding our politics, smothering our relationships, and dampening our own personal happiness. I'm something of a lonely libertarian myself. I've been told on more than one occasion that I'm too conservative for the rigid "anything goes" libertines of my movement, but also far too liberal in how I see the role of government. Which is as much as to say, I think the government should in fact do things and be good at it. Then again, maybe you don't want to listen to someone from the other side of the political divide advise you about how to live, and that's fine.

But what about Star Wars?

Embedded just beneath the surface of this beloved story of adventures in the stars is a message of hope that could light our way out of this tunnel. The characters and core themes of Star Wars offer lessons on living that, if taken as more than just fantasy, offer a real blueprint for having a happier life and healthier politics. These intergalactic tales, whether we encounter them on the big screen, TV, or on bookshelves, consistently revolve around the importance of empathy, humility, courage, hope, redemption, balance, and choice.

At the end of every chapter in this book, you'll find some advice on simple ways you can put these Star Wars virtues into practice in your life. Talk is cheap. Taking action on this stuff is anything but easy. But it's worth it. After all, the "quick and easy path" leads toward the dark side.

We must take the Star Wars story as more than a mere suggestion about how to live.

If we do, the Force can fix the world.

CHAPTER 1

A CHILD QUEEN
AND A WORLD DIVIDED

"Truly wonderful, the mind of a child is."

—Yoda

HUMILITY

IMAGINE YOU'RE A CHILD QUEEN, barely a teenager. Invaders have taken over your whole planet. With each minute that passes, your people are dying, and you have no chance of fighting back without some kind of outside assistance or a major military alliance. Your best hope is in an alien species that you know holds your people in contempt, and also blames *you* for the entire crisis at hand.

Welcome to Star Wars, *Episode I: The Phantom Menace* (1999).

You just took a walk in the petite shoes of Queen Padmé Amidala Naberrie, the young ruler of the prosperous, beautiful, and peaceful world of Naboo. Padmé had reached the end of the line and felt the stinging limitations of her own abilities to save Naboo from occupation by the droid armies of the Trade Federation. After a narrow escape from the clutches of these corporatist creeps on Naboo, thanks to Jedi guardians Obi-Wan Kenobi and Qui-Gon Jinn, Padmé sought a humanitarian intervention from the Galactic Republic. Her hopes were dashed. Politics and diplomacy, much to Padmé's surprise, would not save her people.

Padmé would need a different kind of help, which she hadn't properly considered before. She needed Jar Jar Binks and the Gungans, a warrior race of tall, gangly, human-frog hybrids who lived inside a civilization of underwater bubbles. Star Wars can be wonderfully strange sometimes. Padmé would approach this pivotal moment in the Star Wars saga with an air of grace, service, and humility that would alter the course of galactic history.

This chapter looks at the story of Padmé and the lesson her story offers about how humility can salvage relationships, unite fractured nations, and expand what is possible in politics at a time when all the powers that be want you to believe that you are always, undoubtedly, right.

CHECKMATE

Have you felt a disturbance in the Force? Something has changed in the character of our leaders, family, friends, and foes alike. Everyone seems so sure of themselves, so confident in their opinions, and increasingly reluctant to give ground in debate. Think of the last time you were in a political feud on Facebook and your sparring partner, perhaps a friend from school or a relative, changed their opinion on the matter at hand. If your social media experience is anything like my own, that would be a rarity, to say the least.

In these public clashes, people dig in. One combatant rushes to Google to search for articles, op-eds, academic material, or any statistic that might back up their argument. Once they find something, it gets hurled into the comments section like some sort of intellectual checkmate. Whenever I see this happen, I usually assume the perpetrator didn't actually read the material they've found, but instead are hoping that their deployment of favorable "evidence" will be enough to diffuse the debate and cow their friend or opponent into submission.

This is how it works. We know this because we've all done it, on or off social media. Why is it so scary for people to just say, "I don't know"?

It feels good to be right. Knowing that, it's not particularly surprising that we have manufactured a society that reinforces, in realms ranging from social media to the service industry to the evening news, the idea that "the customer is always right." Of course, we know that this is not the case. People are wrong all the time. But whether it's a hotel dealing with an upset guest or cable news reporting on the latest insanity in Washington, it's not a great business model to challenge your customers, fans, subscribers, or even your *voters* head-on.

FIGHTING THE FORCE OF FACEBOOK

The human brain can be wired and rewired in all sorts of ways. Observers of politics who are older than I might look back to the popularization of talk radio and Rush Limbaugh as the start of the echo chambers that took hold of American political debate. My mind always goes to 2011, when Facebook announced yet another remodel of the News Feed. The News Feed of Facebook is where all the action happens, and when it was created in 2006 the Feed was chronological. It made the Facebook experience a bit of a crapshoot. If your child or sibling posted a major life update to the News Feed in 2006, such as getting engaged, a few hours before you logged in—you might have missed it. This was an imperfect system, no doubt.

Between 2008 and 2010, Facebook started to let predictive algorithms govern what appeared on a user's feed, supposedly to fix stuff like the aforementioned problem about the parent not being able to see the news about their child getting engaged. The computerized algorithm would try to show you what you wanted to see based on familial connections and other inter-personal factors. But it was in 2011 that Facebook updated the system to serve users content in their News Feed that matched their behaviors on the platform. What news are you clicking on, what kind of photos do you tend to "like," which of your friends do you tend to converse with the most? Facebook became reori-ented toward giving the user exactly what a computer would sur-mise they wanted. And just like that, two billion people across the world began to have their sense of self rewired and their self-assurance inflated.

If you're politically liberal and tend to click on articles from the *Washington Post*, the *New York Times*, or CNN, you'll see more of that on your feed and less of content that might represent a different perspective. Articles from Fox News, The Daily Wire, or the *Wall Street Journal*—even if shared by a close friend—likely won't be *prioritized* for you. Instead of Facebook showing you the world as it is happening, it instead shows you the world that you want to see.

This is good business for Facebook, since the goal is to increase the time its users spend on the platform, boosting profits brought in by hungry advertisers. It is a huge problem, however, for the rest of us. Facebook isn't the only social media platform in the game, and while not all of these platforms are programmed to feed our biases, informational echo chambers don't need algorithms to take hold of our lives.

"TOO SURE OF THEMSELVES THEY ARE"

We need an intervention to liberate us from our culture of pride and self-assuredness. This arrogance epidemic is what led Duke University psychologist Mark Leary to develop a series of studies in 2017 on the components of "intellectual humility."[*] He found that when he asked a subject about specific disagreements they'd had with someone in the last six months—using the question "What percentage of the time do you think that you were right?"—it came out to roughly 66 percent. Fewer than half thought they could've been wrong in a majority of disputes.

---

[*] Mark R. Leary, "Cognitive and Interpersonal Features of Intellectual Humility," Duke University, March 17, 2017, https://journals.sagepub.com/doi/abs/10.1177/01461 67217697695.

This kind of attitude pervades our culture across gender, age groups, and political identities.

When Obi-Wan Kenobi mentioned to Yoda in *Episode II: Attack of the Clones* (2002) that his student, Anakin, had a tendency to be arrogant, Yoda laughed. "A flaw more and more common among Jedi. Too sure of themselves they are," he said, and then turned his convicting gaze to Kenobi. "Even the older, more experienced ones."

Yoda's balanced reaction to Obi-Wan reminds me that boastfulness is not exactly a new cross-generational problem. However, when you take the research Leary did and apply it to issues of national importance, such as the 2019 impeachment inquiry against President Trump, it becomes quite troubling.

An NPR/PBS NewsHour/Marist poll asked 988 registered voters, "Can you imagine any information or circumstances during the impeachment inquiry where you might change your mind about your position on impeachment?" Only 25 percent of Democrats indicated they were open to new information that would change their view on Trump's guilt, regarding the assertion that he suppressed military aid to Ukraine to pressure it into launching a corruption investigation into former vice president Joe Biden and his son, Hunter Biden. Republicans surveyed were no better. Only 24 percent of Republicans affirmatively believed that new information from the congressional investigation would change their minds.

How long can we continue to be a free people with democratic norms and a deliberative justice system if the pursuit of truth plays second fiddle to partisan identity? Star Wars has an interesting answer to how intellectual humility can interact with politics. I told you about the story of Queen Padmé Amidala, so let's look a bit closer at this master class in applied humility.

A CHILD QUEEN AND A WORLD DIVIDED

You might recall a scene from *Episode II: Attack of the Clones* (2002) where the now former queen turned senator, Padmé Amidala, and Jedi knight Anakin Skywalker are arriving on Naboo to begin her time in hiding. She needs to lie low and wait out a credible threat of assassination made against her. While reflecting on her time as queen, Padmé says to her Jedi guardian, "I wasn't the youngest queen ever elected. But now that I think back on it, I'm not sure I was old enough. I'm not sure I was ready."

Anakin points out that Padmé had been an overwhelmingly popular queen. He alludes to an effort by the people of Naboo to amend their own constitution in hopes of extending her reign as the elected monarchical ruler of the serene world we see rocked by war in the preceding Star Wars film, *Episode I: The Phantom Menace* (1999).

Padmé was just fourteen years old at the time of the Trade Federation's unprovoked invasion of the peaceful and opulent world of Naboo, a mature democratic society with a peculiar quirk in its system. As if fourteen were not young enough, apparently Padmé wasn't even the youngest queen to sit atop the throne. While we don't know which of her predecessors Padmé was referencing as having been even younger, we do know one of her successors, Queen Apailana (seen only at Padmé's funeral in *Episode III: Revenge of the Sith* [2005]), is merely twelve years old. So this quick exchange between Padmé and Anakin raises a few legitimate questions about the judgment of the good people of Naboo.

Why would any society use the legitimizing power of democratic elections to give executive power to children? We're all somewhat familiar with historical examples of child monarchs who were anointed as heads of state at a young age, thanks to what's known as hereditary monarchies.

For example, King Tut became a pharaoh of Egypt at just age nine. Likewise, Queen Isabella II of Spain was named queen when she was just three years old, only to take the throne officially at age thirteen after a series of civil wars were fought in a failed attempt to prevent a woman from leading the country. Mary, Queen of Scots was merely a toddler when she became queen of Scotland and would go on to challenge Queen Elizabeth I for the English crown, unsuccessfully. There was King Alfonso XIII, age sixteen upon taking the throne of Spain in 1902. He would lead Spain through the 1918 Spanish Flu pandemic and World War I.

The list of real-world child monarchs really does go on and on.

It's truly a marvel of history and somewhat sobering that in all of human existence only recently has it become an oddity to enshrine children with actionable political power. I love my daughter, and she possesses a great deal of intuition and intellectual curiosity for a fifth grader, but I wouldn't voluntarily opt to run her as a candidate for higher office. She lacks wisdom and experience for such a role. The toughest choice she has to make on a daily basis is between packing a sandwich for school or rolling the dice on sometimes very sketchy cafeteria food. There's little reason for me to believe my child is ready to make decisions of life and death in the event a droid army from space invades our little Washington, DC, suburb.

Padmé, at the age of fourteen, did have to make such decisions of consequence.

Following the invasion of her planet, the young queen had to decide whether or not to flee Naboo in pursuit of a political intervention by the Galactic Republic. While she was off-world, Padmé received word from a close advisor, Governor Sio Bibble, that the death toll within Federation-occupied areas of Naboo was "catastrophic." Having already made a desperate plea to the Republic on the floor of the Senate, with no signs of an intervention being forthcoming, Padmé was faced with the decision to return to Naboo and fight the Trade Federation head-on. It was a defining moment for the queen, who with all of her high-minded ideals about democracy and the Republic of which Naboo was a part, had to face an ugly truth. She abandoned the political pursuit of an intervention and got to work on forging a new military alliance to save her people.

Recognizing the Republic's incapacity to come to Naboo's aid was not Padmé's crowning achievement during the crisis on her home planet. Padmé's moment of defining leadership and political vision came when she returned to the planet's surface and realized that the Naboo had a more existential problem to solve if the Trade Federation would ever be driven away by force. Naboo, for all its beauty and elegance, was a world divided.

Say what you will about Jar Jar Binks and the fact that he's a tad annoying, but he is far from unimportant in the grand scheme of the Star Wars story. Risking everything, Padmé asked the *ever-popular* Binks to take her to the leader of the Gungans, Boss Rugor Nass. When Padmé and Binks eventually found the Gungans, they were hiding in the woods, their cities captured and laid to waste by droids. Padmé had a choice to make. She could exploit the Gungans' tenuous situation in hiding to try to convince them that an alliance with her would be in their best interests, and dictate the terms of such an alliance, or she could do the opposite—a somewhat radical proposition for a young ruler aiming to show strength in a crisis.

THE RADICALISM OF BENDING A KNEE

Padmé took the radical approach, which was to display total humility in the eyes of a distrustful and bitter Boss Nass. Leading with the acknowledgment of the equal greatness of their cultures, Padmé took a knee before Nass and said, "I ask you to help us. No, I beg you to help us. We are your humble servants. Our fate is in your hands."

Let that sink in for a moment.

What Queen Padmé Amidala did there was incredibly bold,

so much so that Boss Nass laughed at the very sight of it while the Naboo remained kneeling before him in hopes of an alliance.

Nass's response stunned the bystanders, who already appeared bewildered by Padmé's approach to diplomacy. He said to Queen Amidala in the glorious dialect of the Gungan people, "Yousa no tinken yousa greater den da Gungans? Mesa like dis. Maybe wesa…bein' friends."

Translated for those of you who are not up to speed on Gunganese, that would mean, "You don't think you're greater than the Gungans? I like this. Maybe we can be friends." If you're not familiar with the geopolitics of the planet of Naboo, here's a crash course.

The planet of Naboo features two primary groups of inhabitants. Living underwater in massive technologically advanced cities are the amphibious people known as the Gungans. They're tall, lean, and muscular creatures with thick rubbery skin and faces that blend the likeness of catfish with that of ducks.

With Jar Jar Binks as the leading representative of the Gungan people, you might not know that Gungans are considered a warrior race. They don't revel in violence. The Gungans treasure peace and nonaggression among their principles. Their traditions mirror what you might see in some of the indigenous tribes of our own world. The Gungan way, whether it is waging war or building cities, is to achieve a certain simpatico relationship with the natural world. You can see it on display throughout *Episode I: The Phantom Menace* (1999) in the blue, bubble-like technologies of the Gungans. Their underwater cities, defensive shields on land, and grenades are all derived from natural resources within Naboo's planetary crust.

Take a wild guess as to who disrupted the Gungans' otherwise peaceful and eco-friendly lifestyle. You can have a hint: in the words of Boss Nass, "Dey think dey so smarty, dey think dey brains so big…" That's right! Those dreaded hipster colonists, the Naboo. As Star Wars lore has explained it, the Naboo people first appeared on the planet after fleeing war and strife off-world. When they settled aboveground, hostilities quickly arose—and then boiled over.

It's not clear what started the feud between the Naboo and the Gungans, but it doesn't take an intergalactic Sherlock Holmes to look at the picture George Lucas painted of Naboo and surmise what happened. At some point before the Star Wars films take place, the Gungans were put upon by these human refugees and in the end were driven under the waters of Naboo to live in relative isolation. The two great civilizations, while deeply resentful of one another, lived apart in peace.

LEADERSHIP AND LISTENING

What I've just described is the cold war that effectively ended when Queen Amidala bent the knee before the Gungan people to ask for their help. It was a gambit that paid off with the defeat of the Trade Federation and liberation of their shared planet.

The old proverb "The enemy of my enemy is my friend" maintains its relevance over time and space. But to chalk off what happened on Naboo to a simple handshake agreement between civilizations in order to defeat a common enemy would really miss the point.

The Gungans and the Naboo didn't just defeat the Trade Federation and go back to their lives. Jar Jar Binks was made a junior senator for the planet, going on to corepresent the world in the Galactic Senate, next to Padmé, when she entered that next phase of her political career. This was the first-ever Gungan involvement in galactic affairs. Their entire existence was transformed in those few harrowing days known as the Naboo Crisis, but this would prove to be the canary in the coal mine of a coming civil war that would engulf the entire galaxy.

So I ask you again: why would the Naboo elect children as their leaders?

Well, the Naboo understand that leadership and listening are one and the same. The home world of Padmé Amidala has an interesting political system, to say the least. The Naboo elect a monarch who serves two years at a time, with a maximum of two terms. These individuals are usually exceptionally young, they are usually female, and they come from elite families. Young talent for civil service is groomed within Naboo's Royal Academy of Government, again referenced in passing by Padmé in *Episode II: Attack of the Clones* (2002).

These young leaders are surrounded by a cohort of more seasoned administrators, known as the Royal Advisory Council, and they have authority over domestic affairs, while managing galactic politics falls to Naboo's senators. Those senators that represent the planet within the Galactic Republic are appointed by the monarch, making them more akin to the United Nations ambassadors of our own world.

The Naboo clearly place a high value on the intuitions of their young people, while maintaining a respect for the age and experience that is reflected in the Advisory Council. When I think of children at their best, they are champions of curiosity, adaptability, openness, and, above all, humility.

PUT YOUR LISTENING EARS ON

For instance, there's a reason kids are superior when it comes to learning new languages early in their life. Children learn unconsciously, as if their default setting is to absorb and redeploy information. Adults, on the other hand, because they have so much more to manage in their minds (bills, schedules, work, raising kids), have to consciously shift into a state of mind for learning. According to UCLA neurology professor Paul Thompson, children have a particularly powerful asset in the deep motor area of the brain that governs these unconscious actions. Before children reach age eleven, the centers in the brain responsible for language are growing rapidly, and picking up a new language is easier.* It's a subtle difference, but most adults know that "going along to get along" is just a way of life at a certain age.

---

* Paul Thompson, "UCLA Researchers Map Brain Growth in Four Dimensions, Revealing Stage-Specific Growth Patterns in Children," UCLA, March 8, 2000, https://users.loni .usc.edu/~thompson/MEDIA/press_release.html.

There's also the matter of inhibition. There is such a thing as a shy child, but for the most part, kids don't begin their life with stage fright. Children don't lose sleep over mispronouncing a word or attempting to explain something while getting tongue-tied along the way. Put simply, self-consciousness is learned later in life. Related to this cocktail of negativity, learning a second language later in life is far more fraught with anxiety. Once you speak your native language fluently, there's a mental hurdle most have to clear to learn a new language. What's in it for me? Will this take time away from other activities I enjoy? What will my friends think of me learning this? Issues ranging from practical concerns over time to more societal constraints like the stigma around bilingual speakers are less likely to concern the average child.

Extrapolate that to how a child might engage in politics. Right off the bat, you'd have someone who approaches governance with curiosity and a natural interest in problem-solving. They would have no assumptions about their greatness or mastery of the universe. There's no shortage of moving parts in politics, which is presumably where a Royal Advisory Council comes into play for a young monarch on Naboo. The trick is how you interpret the incoming information shared by your advisors.

My challenge to you is the same as it would be to a monarch like Padmé: remember and cherish the number-one favorite word of children. That word is "why."

Children ask, "Why?" And they do it a lot. Without shame or apprehension, they ask for more information at every turn. It can be frustrating at times to be on the receiving end of that question, but you miss it when it's gone. People tend to stop asking questions as they get older, either to minimize conflict or to lie low at school or the workplace, or they've developed some certainty—about who they are, what they know, and what they can do.

Those two approaches manifest themselves in the ethos of "fake it to make it," a somewhat learned behavior that comes from a place of social pressure, real or perceived, to present yourself as competent. Then there's "hubris," meaning to have excessive pride or self-confidence. Both of these are exactly what Naboo is seeking to weed *out* of its political talent pool. They want leaders who will question, seek knowledge, admit when they're wrong, and adapt to do better. Can you think of any world leaders, perhaps of a democratic nation, whose entire ethos is built around intense ego and an air of infallibility?

CONFIDENCE VERSUS PRIDE

"Truly I tell you, unless you change and become like little children, you will never enter the kingdom of heaven. Therefore, whoever humbles himself like this little child is the greatest in the kingdom of heaven."

—Matthew 18:3–4

Jesus Christ was a fan of humility, going so far as to lecture a room full of his followers about it. Christ himself was something of a case study in modesty. After all, he was a carpenter-king born in a manger while still being on track to inherit the King-dom of Heaven and sit at the right hand of God. But his per-sonal biography was not why Christ valued humility.

The thirteenth-century philosopher St. Thomas Aquinas is credited with saying, "Humility removes pride, whereby a man refuses to submit himself to the truth of faith." Pride is indeed a human vice, and considered by many theologians to be the most poisonous of the so-called seven deadly sins: lust, gluttony, greed, sloth, wrath, envy, and pride.

C. S. Lewis believed pride to be the sin from which all oth-ers flow,* because by its very definition it is a state of mind that hides the existence of your own wrongdoing. Pride is the mir-ror we hold up to ourselves to glorify our own achievements, thoughts, and deeds.

What Boss Nass disdained in the Naboo wasn't their art, their architecture, or their clothes. The problem wasn't the way they looked. It was that "they think they're so smart, they think their brains so big." It was the snobby attitude of the Naboo that Nass and the Gungans resented.

If you've ever turned on Fox News during the weekend of the Academy Awards, then you've heard their anchors and guests rail against the "Hollywood elites." Maybe you've spent time in a small town nowhere near a major metropolitan area. If so, you've probably heard an older person denounce "city slickers" before.

---

* C. S. Lewis, *The Screwtape Letters*, reprint ed. (1942; repr., San Francisco, CA: HarperOne, 2015).

The term is a little dusty at this point, but the same idea applies to chiding "hipsters" for moving into your town and bringing their kombucha bars with them. In both directions what is so grating is the pride, the condescension, and the contempt.

The thing that's so tricky about pride is that no one wants to discourage someone, like a child, from being confident or believing in themselves. That would foster an insecurity that can be ugly in its own right. The difference is that confidence is the understanding of your own abilities, as well as your own deficiencies. I can't be confident in my abilities as a writer unless I understand the feeling that algebra has given me since middle school—a cold chill down my spine.

Pride, on the other hand, is taking one's achievements and consistently ascribing them to yourself. It would be me writing this very chapter and thinking with great self-satisfaction, "What a master of the written word I am," when in reality I was instructed by teachers and mentors throughout my life and developed an aptitude that I had for the craft. Even further, there's a difference between saying, "I have a talent" versus "I have a gift." To have a gift means that someone, or something, gave it to you.

LET GO, AND LET THE FORCE

In the Christian tradition, a follower of Christ believes they need a savior. But would a deeply prideful person really think they need saving by a power they cannot see, hear, or touch? Doubtful. You could think of that person as Han Solo. This kind of person thrives because in their mind they think they know how the world works, and they survive by grit mixed with a little good luck. That's why Han in *Episode IV: A New Hope* (1977) is so quick to dismiss the existence of the Force and deride Obi-Wan Kenobi's "hokey religion." A blaster, good aim, and street smarts have always been Han's salvation, and to him, the sight of Luke Skywalker covering his own eyes to train with Obi-Wan is the definition of naïveté

Toward the end of the film, when Luke famously pilots the trench of the Death Star to deliver the shot heard round the galaxy, Luke again covers his eyes—figuratively. The voice of Obi-Wan reaches out to him with the advice Luke needs to make a nearly impossible shot: "Use the Force, Luke. Let go." So Luke turns off his targeting computer and fires his rockets in an act of faith, practically blind. It is naïve, but it is also inspired, because the Death Star operation was, in fact, a nearly impossible mission.

Luke couldn't make that shot. No one could. So Luke let the Force take the shot for him, and he made a believer of Han Solo that day.

Perhaps Luke derived this sensibility unwittingly from his long-lost mother, Padmé. She approached political diplomacy with an openness and vulnerability Christ himself might have prescribed, which is to say she knew the Naboo needed help. When she said to Nass, "Our fate is in your hands," that is the essence of being childlike. You live each day knowing you're dependent on others to survive. When Jesus asked his followers to be more like children, he wasn't calling on them to be dupes.

No, not at all. In chapter ten he said to them, "I am sending you out like sheep among wolves. Therefore, be as shrewd as snakes and as innocent as doves" (Matthew 10:16). Padmé was as shrewd as a snake, but also gentle enough as a queen to submit when the time was right.

ACCEPT AND VALUE CHALLENGE

Challenge makes us stronger. It helps us strengthen our understanding of the world and the problems we face. Being confronted regularly with new perspectives, counterfactuals, and even inconvenient information is how we make the most constructive decisions of our lives. But is that possible without some semblance of humility?

Based on everything we've discussed here, sure, it's possible, but it's a heck of a lot harder. I told you at the start of this chapter how the world is increasingly oriented toward the adage of "The customer is always right," and I want you to know that nothing could be further from the truth. *Search your feelings. You know it to be true.*

Rush Limbaugh did more than just tell his audience that he was always right. No, he was far more clever during his time ruling the talk radio airwaves. Rush always made sure to compliment his listeners and remind them that they were the smartest audience in the world. "They already know the truth," he'd say. "El Rushbo" was simply there to affirm what they already knew. And the feedback loop goes round and round.

The story of Padmé and the crisis on Naboo is a story of how having humility can create new avenues for action and make problem-solving all the more possible. It's a story of knowing what you don't know, and a story of living in a state of openness to new information, new friends, and new outcomes. Having all the talent and political chops in the galaxy isn't worth a thing if you aren't able to see your limits.

Don't just know your limitations; own them. Make an effort to learn more, and surround yourself with people who fill in certain gaps. If you don't, whether it be in your work or at trivia night with friends at the pub, your limitations will multiply.

Tips: How to Build Humility

- **It is okay to *not* have an opinion about everything.** You can only know so much, and we should focus on knowing a lot about the things we're passionate about.

- **Say what you don't know.** If you want to have better conversations and political debates, then share what you are *unsure* of just as loudly as you affirm what you believe to be true. This opens up more space for conversation and discovery between both parties. When someone enters a debate, they are in the defensive crouch. If you want to really *talk*, first you must draw them out of that crouch. Displaying intellectual humility is a powerful method for doing this.

- **You don't have to quit social media.** But for every Facebook page or opinionated social media account you follow that aligns neatly with your point of view, follow two more that challenge your patience and boundaries daily. Seeing what your political opposites are reading and concerned with will help *you* know what fights are coming, and how to change minds when they come.

- **Know the game.** Understand that what you're watching is meant to incense and reinforce the viewpoints and bias of a strategically chosen audience. Bookmark websites like the *Columbia Journalism Review* (www.cjr.org) and keep up with their reporting on the political news media just as much or more than you consume cable news.

- **Take a trip.** Go somewhere completely unfamiliar. Getting a dose of wonder in your life every so often helps to keep your outlook large and your sense of self in check. Being somewhere new means you'll need the help of others to make the most of the experience.

CHAPTER 2

A CREATURE IN
A MASK

"Keep your concentration here and now
where it belongs."

—Qui-Gon Jinn

EMPATHY

REY HAD NOWHERE TO GO. She'd been captured by Kylo Ren, the ghoulish villain we first meet in Star Wars *Episode VII: The Force Awakens* (2015) during a battle on the forest planet of Takodana.

"You still want to kill me," Kylo says to her in his garbled robotic voice, filtered by the mask he wears. "That happens when you're being hunted by a creature in a mask," Rey snaps back at him.

What happens next has always struck me when I watch *The Force Awakens*. Ren says nothing. He simply steps back from Rey, reaches for his helmet, and pulls it off, slamming it down on the table next to them with a crashing thud. Rey looks bewildered and suddenly uncomfortable in a way her being held captive doesn't quite explain. Ren is human. He's a young man (handsome too). This frightful character was not some "ghoul," and he wasn't that different from Rey. Her eyes flittered, and she squinted. Was this really what was beneath the mask of Kylo Ren?

Have you had that kind of experience before? A moment where your perception of a person or group was shattered in an instant by some act of vulnerability or humility and suddenly the person who stood before you was not a monster, but a person? I hope you have. But if I'm being honest, those moments are harder and harder to come by in a world increasingly ordered by "user preference." Empathy is basically one person's ability to understand or relate to the feelings of another. It's a value that goes beyond teaching your kids how to make friends on the playground. Empathy is more important to society at large than just providing married couples a tool with which to navigate conflict.

Empathy is a fundamental ingredient of a democracy. It's how we relate to people that are unlike us on the surface but with whom we still find common cause. The only kind of society where you don't have to worry about how other people may feel about things is a dictatorship, because only one person's feelings matter in *that* scenario. More important, empathy lends to humanizing our opponents and resisting the gravitational pull of tribal politics, which demands that we reduce political opposites to something other than complex individuals. Star Wars has numerous stories of empathy that intertwine with the goal of creating a more free and open galaxy, of respecting the individual. Whether it's encounters with alien species or confronting villains shielded by menacing masks, the journey of any hero in the Star Wars universe tends to involve a personal quest for empathy. Sometimes it comes easily, like Princess Leia and her immediate connection with the fuzzy Ewoks on the planet Endor in *Return of the Jedi* (1983). Other times it's a monumental challenge, as with Rey's struggle against Kylo Ren. In a world where the powerful want to limit your cognitive ability to relate to others and build unlikely friendships or bonds of affection, empathy is a rebellious quality. More empathy could help fix the world.

REBEL SCUM

Cockroaches. Rats. Parasites. Meat bags. Clones. Rebel scum. You've probably heard at least one of these slurs thrown around on the big screen to describe human beings in iconic movies that leave a mark you can't soon forget. *Hotel Rwanda* (2004), a well-known drama depicting the 1994 Rwandan ethnic genocide against the Tutsis by an ethnic majority called the Hutus, was where I remember hearing "cockroaches" uttered over a radio broadcast calling Hutus to take up arms and slaughter any and every Tutsi they could find. I was just about fifteen years old when my church youth group hosted a viewing of that movie for the express purpose of discussing what it means to be human. Rats, or *untermenschen*, may be what you picked up from *Schindler's List* (1993) or your high school studies of World War II and the Nazi-led Holocaust of Jews, Gypsies, and other minority populations deemed less than human by Hitler's regime. Soviet propagandists in Stalin's Russia penned pamphlets describing their German foes as "two-legged animals who have mastered the technique of war."

Whether it's criminal violence or within the confines of war, empathy is a liability. Seeing yourself in others or feeling what they feel is a barrier that must be "overcome."

Well-meaning people learn about high-profile instances of mass atrocity and evil and categorize them as something inhuman, deeds that otherwise normal people stumbled into or were tricked into accepting. The tougher truth to grapple with is that humankind is perfectly capable and even wired to do unbelievably wicked things. What makes us unique in the natural world is that humanity is able to build mental and emotional constructs in which doing those things becomes easier to digest. The words we choose have both meaning and great power. They affect the extent to which we need to tap into our reserves of empathy.

Do you ever wonder how in Star Wars the people of the Republic were able to stomach the brutality of the Clone Wars? It was a conflict that resulted in millions upon millions of deaths in the war against the Separatists' droid armies. What did the Republic do to face down the threat in *Episode II: Attack of the Clones* (2002)? The Galactic Senate sanctioned the creation of a clone army. Those clones, created on an assembly line in a cutting-edge factory from the DNA of one Jango Fett, were born in test tubes and raised to fight—and die for the Republic.

It's really quite horrific. The supposed "good guys" of the Star Wars prequel trilogy bred human life for the purpose of throwing those bodies into the gears of war. These weren't "people" to Republic bureaucrats or even some in the Jedi Order; they were just "clones." There are few instances during the movie when the inherent individuality of these soldiers is recognized.

It's no wonder a society this decadent morphed so seamlessly into being the Galactic Empire.

Despite all of its imperfection and fraught history, the United States stands as a beacon of democracy and pluralism to the rest of the world. It's a position that America has earned through trial, through failure, and by right of just how radical the American experiment is. A multiracial democracy, a constitution predicated on individual rights in opposition to the whims of the collective, rights that are endowed by a creator and not the government—these are uniquely American values. Heck, America is one of only a few countries in the world with no official language. It's a beautiful and incredibly challenging thing we're doing here.

What ties it all together is a somewhat tedious and unspoken truth, which is that because America is built on the value of debate, difference, and deference...we aren't always going to like one another. But we're stuck with each other. The alternatives have been tried and are vicious, ugly, and dehumanizing. We're all here in this American republic, hoping to be heard, to be seen, to be recognized, and to have our basic needs, such as security, love, and belonging, met by our fellow citizens.

Empathy helps us to connect with those unlike us, to walk in their shoes, and hopefully in so doing—to reach consensus. That's politics, after all, consensus and compromise. When there's a conflict and politics is no longer on the table, we call that war.

THE DARK SIDE CLOUDS EVERYTHING

Something is happening in American politics. The lines are getting blurred between acceptable and unacceptable discourse, between political affiliations that are within the bounds of the great debate and those that are existentially dangerous.

During the January 6, 2021, riot at the US Capitol building, in which Trump supporters mobbed the building and ransacked the halls of Congress, one Ashli Babbitt was shot dead by Hill police while trying to get into a secure area. She bled out from the neck as people around her screamed. Babbitt was a well-documented supporter of the QAnon conspiracy theory that alleges the Democratic Party and State Department are in cahoots to exploit and traffic children around the world, in addition to engaging in satanic blood rituals. She died in the company of some deeply unsavory characters, white nationalists and right-wing militants among them. Conspiracy theories make for strange bedfellows. Whether the participants are evangelical pastors or committed neo-Nazis, the QAnon theory has the power to unite them around a shared cause: defeating an evil and subhuman cabal of enemies. It's a deadly scary movement and one predicated on abandoning empathy for your political opponents in favor of the mantle of quasi-spiritual heroism.

Did Ashli Babbitt deserve to die? My view is that if you storm the US Capitol you certainly shouldn't be *surprised* by the use of deadly force. But deserving it is something else entirely. If you were so unfortunate as to have been on Twitter the following day, you could find a wealth of conviction in comments from people who'd never met Babbitt who were quite certain she did deserve it. Arthur Chu, an eleven-time winner of the TV game show *Jeopardy*, now a political columnist, took to Twitter on January 7 to say the following regarding Babbitt's death: "When a bullet goes through the fatty tumor a Nazi has in the space where a human being would have a brain, nothing is lost" (@arthur_affect).* Naturally, this tweet and the thread that came after it have since been deleted by Chu. Curious minds can easily find images of the tweets online from before they were wiped away.

To keep this simple and not get mired in the unknown, we can summarize Babbitt's involvement as follows: Babbitt was not known to have any neo-Nazi or white supremacist affiliations. She was in a mob that included some of those people. From what we know, she was a Trump Republican and a conspiracy theorist. What worries me about Chu's statements here, beyond

---

* Lauryn Overhultz, "Former 'Jeopardy!' Champion Arthur Chu Calls Death Of Woman At Capitol One Of The 'Good Things' About The Riots," Daily Caller, January 7, 2021, https://dailycaller.com/2021/01/07/arthur-chu-ashli-babbitt-death-nazi-good-thing-capitol-protest-twitter-jeopardy/.

the graphic dehumanization of a stranger and the supposed righteousness in doing so, is that there was zero burden of proof required to apply the label of "Nazi" to Babbitt and by extension mark her for death.

I'll just say it—I have been a called "Nazi" and "fascist" more times by strangers than I can count. Why? Because those are just slurs that young Republicans learn to endure from their most thoughtless opponents on the Left—a lesson I learned as soon as I was old enough to knock on doors for Mitt Romney's 2012 campaign. My own brother (whom I adore) has playfully chided me about my more conservative stances, calling them fascistic in years past, because he's pretty Far Left. I used to joke back that he and his anarcho-punk friends saw a Nazi around every corner, and even under their own beds at night. I know (many) self-identified Republicans, even Libertarians, get pegged with that moniker indiscriminately and are angrily accustomed to it, despite it being unfounded and untrue 99.9 percent of the time.

That being the case, do Arthur Chu and the thousands of people who retweeted and liked his murderous rant feel authorized to kill *me*? Or certain members of my family who'd call themselves conservative? Or some of my friends who have unfortunately fallen victim to this QAnon madness and voted for Trump?

"To a dark place this line of thought will carry us," Yoda said to his Jedi colleagues in *Episode III: Revenge of the Sith* (2005) as they gathered round a briefing room table to discuss the possibility of removing Chancellor Palpatine from office—by force.

I bring that up not because the Jedi needed to pause and empathize with their treacherous chancellor, but because they decided the gravity of the situation superseded the necessity to respond with democratic methods and process.

In this galaxy we live in, empathy and a shared sense of both humanity and common purpose are what stand between democracy and—well, everything else.

WHAT'S ZAPPING OUR EMPATHY?

The immediate problem we face as a society is that numerous studies in recent years have shown that empathy is on the decline. In 2010 Sara H. Konrath released a study through the University of Michigan that found college students' sense of empathy for others had declined nearly 40 percent between the 1970s and the 2000s.* Empathy here was measured on a scale involving both "empathic concern" and "perspective taking," so the study measured the emotional component of sympathy while also capturing a person's ability to see things from another point of view. It's remarkable that as we've all become more "connected" than ever, this research shows us drifting apart in a dramatic way.

A popular scapegoat for this decline is often technology. If you'd asked me before researching this issue, I also probably

---

* Sara H. Konrath, Edward H. O'Brien, and Courtney Hsing, "Changes in Dispositional Empathy in American College Students Over Time," University of Michigan, August 2010, https://www.ipearlab.org/media/publications/Changes_in_Dispositional _Empathy_-_Sara_Konrath.pdf.

would have pointed to phones and social media as the cause of this unfortunate trend. You see it every day if you're online. Friends and family acting toward one another in ways you couldn't imagine them doing in person. Complete strangers making frightening or even threatening remarks in comments sections. Politics is almost always the inciting factor. We tend to think that the barrier social media puts between us and another person brings out this behavior, but the truth is more complicated. In fact, a 2016 study conducted in Denmark was able to show slight increases in empathy among adolescents who used social media.* What Konrath at the University of Michigan points to as driving the decline in empathy, more than anything, is simply the distraction factor, both as it relates to technology and cultural attitudes around things like work–life balance. To make this more concrete, what it means is that we have finite emotional bandwidth—we can only focus on so much. Being bombarded throughout the day with news alerts, comment notifications, and texts from Mom about her arthritis…really takes it out of you. Then when you're faced with something simple like making eye contact with a homeless person on the street, or something difficult, like withholding judgment on a family friend posting nasty QAnon theories online, you're just plum wiped out.

---

* Helen G.M. Vossen and Patti M. Valkenburg, "Do social media foster or curtail adolescents' empathy?" Utrecht University, May 2016, https://www.pattivalkenburg.nl /images/artikelen_pdf/2016_Vossen__Valkenburg_Do_Social_Media_Foster_Empathy .pdf.

There are a handful of useful studies on distraction and empathy that have shown that when two people sit down to have a cup of coffee, just the presence of a cell phone on the table suppresses the substance of the conversation. "Out of sight, out of mind" applies nicely here. Shalini Misra of Virginia Tech looked at this in a 2014 study, and was able to show that participants got to more personal and weighty topics if their cell phones were not visible.* Connection was made that went beyond talking about the weather and simple pleasantries. The phone isn't really the problem; it's everything on the phone that takes you out of the moment, directing your mind to the future instead.

"Keep your concentration here and now where it belongs," says Master Qui-Gon Jinn to a young Obi-Wan Kenobi at the start of *Episode I: The Phantom Menace* (1999).

"But Master Yoda said I should be mindful of the future," Obi-Wan responds.

"Not at the expense of the moment," says Jinn.

Well put.

The other element I mentioned was work–life balance. The struggle for survival can be a significant depressant on a person's capacity to display empathy toward others. On the extreme side of things, you could consider gang members and the daily fight to survive and provide in incredibly poor neighborhoods. The far less dramatic version of this could be whether your national

---

* Shalini Misra, "The iPhone Effect: The Quality of In-Person Social Interactions in the Presence of Mobile Devices," Virginia Tech, July 1, 2014, https://journals.sagepub.com /doi/abs/10.1177/0013916514539755.

culture is geared more toward leisure or work, and what normative boundaries it places between the two. Americans love to work, and while that's a noble trait as far as I'm concerned, there's no doubt that work and the constant pursuit of financial gain dampen empathy over time. The reason isn't that complex. Humans' most basic instinct is to seek security, and money in the bank equals security. While the average American lives a comfortable life in comparison to people in other parts of the world thanks to cheap consumer goods and a market that thrives on competition, 70 percent of Americans also don't have more than $1,000 in savings. Living like that makes every cough your child or spouse gets feel more like an existential crisis than perhaps just a common cold. What if? Could be something else, something awful. Your mind wanders to the bank account, and you realize just how vulnerable your situation really is. It takes a particularly empathetic person to then wake up the next day and head to the soup kitchen in service of others, instead of heading straight to work to put in extra hours for a few more dollars.

Han Solo always comes to mind when I think about someone with a work complex but who has a naturally empathetic personality warring for more influence over his actions. You see it in the ending of the original Star Wars, *Episode IV: A New Hope* (1977), when Han breaks it off with Luke and Leia right before the final battle against the Death Star. He has debts to pay and a bounty on his head, and he needs to sort that out, immediately. Luke is crushed, and tells him the Rebellion needs him. Han walks away—he has his own problems. But of course, right in the nick of time in Luke's moment of need, Han shows up out of nowhere in his ship, the Millennium Falcon, and gives Luke the cover he needs to blow the Death Star to smithereens. We see this same conflict within Han in the 2018 stand-alone film *Solo: A Star Wars Story*, when a younger Han Solo lands himself a haul of a lucrative chemical called coaxium, but the Rebellion also could use it in the fight against the Empire. Han, this kid who has always had nothing but the clothes on his back, won't join the Rebellion…but he gives the Rebellion the coaxium, keeping just enough for himself to place a bet on the Millennium Falcon and win the ship of his dreams in a card game.

Han has struggled his whole life, and while there's a voice inside him inclined toward selfishness and pride in his own sense of self-reliance, he's never been able to quiet that louder voice that relates strongly to the suffering of others. Walking in another person's shoes is not an alien concept to Solo.

BORROWING THOSE SHOES

As I am writing this, Joe Biden has just stepped down from the podium after giving his inaugural address on January 20, 2021. He just became the forty-sixth president of the United States.* In his speech, something stood out to me about the message he

---

* President Joseph R. Biden Jr., "Inaugural Address," January 20, 2021, https://www .whitehouse.gov/briefing-room/speeches-remarks/2021/01/20/inaugural-address -by-president-joseph-r-biden-jr/.

attempted to convey to the nation, and it gets to the heart of this very chapter. It's an expression you've likely heard:

> The answer is not to turn inward, to retreat into competing factions, distrusting those who don't look like you or worship the way you do, or don't get their news from the same sources you do. We must end this uncivil war that pits red against blue, rural versus urban, conservative versus liberal. We can do this if we open our souls instead of hardening our hearts. If we show a little tolerance and humility, and if we're willing to stand in the other person's shoes, as my mom would say, just for a moment, stand in their shoes.

It's a nice idea. In simpler times, this would feel like the kind of message almost anyone would agree with. The problem, of course, is that actions speak louder than words, and when Biden says this, folks on the other side have come prepared with a laundry list of instances when Biden or his liberal allies openly disrespected them or their way of life—or looked down on them. The level of distrust is high.

There's this moment in *Episode I: The Phantom Menace* (1999) when Jedi master Qui-Gon Jinn tells his Padawan, Obi-Wan Kenobi, that he's going back into the city of Mos Espa to wrap up some unfinished business on the planet. Having just liberated Anakin Skywalker from slavery in a bet with his now former owner, Watto, Qui-Gon was intent on bringing the boy along with them on their journey to Coruscant to train him as a Jedi.

Obi-Wan's reaction? "Why do I sense that we've picked up another pathetic life-form?"

Wow. If Obi-Wan were running for president, that might have been his "basket of deplorables" moment, revealing to the galaxy his general scorn for the unenlightened and unwashed masses beyond the glittering towers of Coruscant. He's of course referencing Jar Jar Binks, whom they had also picked up along their travels and was likely annoying him (and certain older members of the Star Wars audience). It's a line delivered as some sort of jest—one shouldn't take Obi-Wan too seriously here— but it reveals a certain aloofness in the young Jedi to the value and struggles of others. Tone-deaf at best, callous and contemptuous at worst.

I don't recall a time I've spoken with a committed Democrat or Republican and they told me, "I absolutely feel respected by the other side." We live in a polarized age in which our partisan news bubbles and echo chambers created by social media feed us stories of open contempt on demand and all the time. The coverage by MSNBC and CNN of states that voted for Trump casts the people in a negative light, as bitter racists and unworthy. After all, they're just "flyover states," so the expression goes, which is a nicer way of asking, "Who would want to land *there*?" After the incident of January 6, 2021, when the US Capitol was stormed and ransacked by a mob of Trump supporters, Anderson Cooper of CNN took to the air and said of them, "They're going to go back to the Olive Garden and to the Holiday Inn that they're staying at, or the Garden Marriott, and they're going to have some drinks and they're going to talk about the great day they had in Washington."*

The message from Cooper here was clear. This New York City liberal broadcaster thought the rioters were trashy (and they were), so obviously they would be having dinner at the most popular Italian-themed chain restaurant in the country, where a family of almost any means can enjoy a white-tablecloth meal, anytime. Even I took moderate offense. When I was just starting my family and money was at its tightest, Olive Garden was a destination, not because the food was particularly great but because going there, being served in a nice environment, having the white tablecloth, made us (mostly me) feel like we were doing okay as parents and providers. Going there is literally about a feeling. Either way, an unfortunate example of empathy being nowhere to be found in our national discourse.

Fox News and Newsmax churn out the opposite, making every instance of absurdity in Portland or on a college campus into a national story about "snowflakes," overly sensitive liberals who can't survive adversity and whose concerns about injustice are therefore moot. The hosts and panelists will convene, discuss the story, laugh, mock, and ridicule city-dwelling millennials or minority activists to the delight of their audience. It's a ritual.

The call by President Biden for Republicans and Democrats to walk in one another's shoes is a worthy one, but not easily

---

* Anne Riley Moffat, "Olive Garden Yanked Into Trump Culture War With CNN Comment," Bloomberg News, January 8, 2021, https://www.bloomberg.com/news/articles /2021-01-08/olive-garden-yanked-into-trump-s-culture-war-with-cnn-comment.

achieved. Empathy is a powerful virtue to practice, and it can move the largest of logjams in a relationship, but what if we struggle to see the person before us as just that...a person? And even worse, what if they don't want you to see them that way? So they hide behind a mask.

MASKS AND WHAT LIES BENEATH

Star Wars has a handful of traditions and themes that you can trace throughout its entire cinematic history. Whether it's the hero who wears white or the villain dressed in black, or the use of music to signal the virtue or evil of any given character, visual and audio symbolism is essential to storytelling in a galaxy far, far away. One of those symbols is masks.

The original trilogy, starting in 1977 with *Episode IV: A New Hope* and continuing with *The Empire Strikes Back* (1980) and *Return of the Jedi* (1983), was mostly made iconic not by its heroes, but by the masked malefactor Darth Vader. Fans were made to wonder for many years about what was beneath the mask. What was the full story of this man whom Obi-Wan derided as being "more machine now than man"?

Beginning in *The Empire Strikes Back*, we start to understand. Vader was once a man named Anakin Skywalker who turned to the dark side and in so doing lost pieces of his humanity along the way. Still, we don't know what literally lies beneath. While Luke Skywalker is training to be a Jedi on the swampy world of Dagobah with the pint-size Master Yoda, he experiences a vision of sorts in which he battles Vader and wins. When Vader falls headless to the ground, his mask bursts open and a face is revealed. It's Luke's face.

Symbolic, of course. We know from this vision that the truth of Vader's identity isn't really the point. It's that Luke, too, could become like Vader if he's not careful with the Force. The mask allows anyone watching Star Wars to put themselves inside the black suit of robotic armor and consider, "This could be me."

Episode VII: The Force Awakens (2015) does something similar. The movie's three main characters are all introduced with their faces covered by masks. When Rey is introduced, she appears masked on the desert planet of Jakku, rummaging through a downed Star Destroyer for scrap parts. We quickly learn she's all alone, abandoned there by a family she barely remembers. Finn, another of these three masked characters, is first introduced as a stormtrooper. He serves in the ranks of the neo-Imperial First Order, a fighting force composed of kidnapped children from all around the galaxy, brainwashed and raised to fight. Finn is snapped out of his brainwashing by a violent trauma. One of his comrades is struck down in battle, and then reaches out with a blood-soaked hand, defacing Finn's mask.

Once he is alone, the stormtrooper, known first by his dehumanizing call sign FN-2187, rips his mask off. What we see is a frightened and upset young man. It's the first time Star Wars audiences have ever had a real look at the human being inside that famous armor.

Then, of course, there's Kylo Ren.

Masks by their nature are hiding something. In some cases, it's something the wearers don't want you to see—ugliness, shame, or maybe truth. Sometimes it's a thing the wearers themselves don't want to see, or maybe would prefer to forget. In other instances, the mask can itself be a new identity to fill the void created by losing your sense of self and becoming something new. One or all of these things can be true, sometimes all at once. We all wear masks, don't we? Probably not in the literal sense, but we're masters of covering up how we feel or who we really are by creating alternate personas to navigate different situations. My wife likes to joke about her "customer service voice" as someone who has worked in the service industry for over a decade. There's a certain elevation of the voice and the use of a manufactured smile that comes along with certain types of jobs. You probably know of a few.

Sometimes we take on harsh masks as well, to avoid vulnerability and opening ourselves up to feeling hurt. A child acting out at school and being cruel to others can be wearing a mask. Sit them down and ask a few questions, and you may uncover a great deal of pain and unhappiness that they're covering up with hostility and faux shows of strength.

MASK UP

So what does this have to do with empathy? A lot, actually. Our challenge as modern people is to be able to recognize the masks, both literal and figurative, that people around us are wearing, and do the hard work of seeing past the masks to the person underneath. It won't always be as easy as Kylo Ren literally removing his mask and humanizing himself before Rey. Let's look at two examples.

ANTIFA! Have I got your attention? I'm not a fan of this violent leftist gang. The idea that young progressives would dress in all black, cover their faces, march with red anarcho-flags, and carry an assortment of melee weapons around the downtowns of major US cities is incredibly disturbing to me. They attack journalists, beat innocent bystanders, vandalize businesses, and, in some cases, have torched government buildings. They do this, of course, all in the name of "antifascism," and thus their name, "Antifa." What's with the masks?

On the surface it's totally tactical. Antifa activists mask their identities because it seems that anytime they get together or mingle, a ton of property damage and violent crime just happens to occur in the process. It's hard to know who is involved with Antifa, and it's hard for federal and local law enforcement to arrest and prosecute participants after the fact when they can't be clearly identified. Simple enough. But I can't help but feel like there's something more going on with these mostly white urbanites who, based on some of their other physical characteristics, look like they just left an art gallery opening before showing up to smash cop cars and punch reporters. I'll just say it—take away the black garb and masks and what's left is mostly kinda wimpy.

With all of their participants dressed in black, makeshift armor, and face coverings, Antifa employs a strategy called "black bloc." Think about what that means, more so than what it is. You get a whole host of people together, get them to dress the same, strip away individual identity, and become one single force. Immediately, you're not just a mob of Portland baristas and record collectors, you're a movement—you're intimidating. Black bloc gives its users anonymity, and thus less accountability, while bringing them together within a collective. Otherwise weak people are made more powerful by the group. It's not a stretch to take that idea across the political spectrum and apply it to the life of the average stormtrooper. In Star Wars, the Empire's recruiting efforts targeted young people in rough-and-tumble corners of the galaxy who saw stormtroopers as warriors and guardians of order. Sign up for the imperial military, wear the armor, don the mask, and fight back against crime and lawlessness in your community.

Don't be a victim—be a stormtrooper. I want to be clear: Antifa and the Empire don't have much in common in terms of ideology. Antifa is closer to communism, whereas the Empire draws more on certain elements of fascism, but the through line is collectivism and the shedding of individual identity in favor of being part of a group. The mask is step one for truly joining that kind of collective, and it's also what your opposition will point to in order to demonize your cause and dehumanize you in the process.

THAT NAME NO LONGER HAS
ANY MEANING FOR ME

Bishop Omar Jahwar was a spiritual activist and community leader in the Dallas–Fort Worth area. Before he tragically passed away in March 2021 from complications related to COVID-19, Jahwar was the presiding bishop of the Kingdom Covenant of Churches and helped found an organization called Urban Specialists. The organization was created to halt violence on the streets of American cities. Gang violence was the primary focus of Omar, who took a hands-on approach to getting to know competing gang leaders in a city and then meeting with them to try to understand them better. Part of Bishop Jahwar's belief, and the logic of Urban Specialists, is that while urban gangs tend to stumble into cycles of perpetual violence, the vast majority of members within these gangs would like to not die violent deaths. They want to live, and, in many cases, they'd like to have new lives that don't involve gangs at all. So his approach was kind of radical. There are plenty of nonprofits dedicated to getting people, mostly young men, out of gangs but there were none focused on simply making the enterprise less violent.

Omar got his start counseling men behind bars who were serving time for all sorts of crime and then aligning themselves with prison gangs. It was there he had this kind of revelation, that while gangs and their foot soldiers are indeed scary to the general public, these are mostly desperate young men trying to survive. In America's most violent neighborhoods, gangs fill a void for destitute families by offering both income for young men of the house and protection by way of affiliation with the gang. For young men lacking stable families to support, the embrace of gangs stands in for the safety that family would normally provide. The cost, however, is high. Bloodshed is almost always involved.

I spoke to Omar in April 2020, and he told me that what he realized when meeting with these men was that they were one person when they were with their gang and another person when they were with him. They had bifurcated their own identities, adopting one sense of self tied to the gang and another that was their private, more authentic self. The trouble is that identities war inside of us for control of the entire being, and after enough compromise, enough unforgettable evil, enough killing...the mask that a young man wears to receive security from a gang can consume him entirely.

The culture of Star Wars' dark side practitioners, the Sith, is eerily similar. When a person commits to the life of a Sith, they take on a new name that begins with "Darth," and, in most cases, the next part of their new name is assigned to them by a master. Their old self is to die with their old name. The young man who grew up on Tatooine, for example, ceases to be "Anakin Skywalker," and becomes Darth Vader. When Vader is confronted by his son, Luke, in *Episode VI: Return of the Jedi* (1983), and addressed by the name Anakin Skywalker, it elicits quite the physical reaction. Vader wheels around, pointing a lightsaber to Luke's chest, and declares, "That name no longer has any meaning for me."

This is exactly the kind of mentality Omar saw all too frequently with young men serving time. A combination of disassociation and hostility to an outstretched hand. The mask they've chosen is protection, from perceived threats both physical and spiritual. Omar's job was to try to see past it, help these young men remove it, and as much as he could—show them the way back to the light.

EMPATHY IS A DANGEROUS NECESSITY

The thing about Kylo Ren is that he really is a broken individual. Beneath the mask, the boy he used to be...Ben Solo...the estranged son of rogue smuggler, Han Solo, and the esteemed Princess Leia, is crying out for an escape hatch out of the darkness he's in. Midway through *Episode VII: The Force Awakens* (2015) we see Kylo huddled in his personal chambers, kneeling over the burnt-up mask of his long-deceased grandfather, Darth Vader, admitting he feels "the pull to the light." He wants out. Soon after we get the scene where he reveals his face for the first time to Rey and the audience, and a connection is made. What comes next immediately tears that brief empathetic moment to shreds.

First there was Kylo invading the sanctity of Rey's mind while she was being held captive. He used the Force to reach inside and see her thoughts and fragmented memories, saying, "I can take whatever I want." A deeply ugly and entitled attitude that for anyone who has ever been victim of an abusive partner might have felt all too familiar. Any empathy you felt upon the mask's removal was diminished.

Then there was the murder of his own father, Han Solo. In a sense, Kylo killed not only his father, but a father figure to millions of fans. He did it because his love for his parents still lived inside of him, and he'd decided it was his greatest weakness. The path to redemption was alluring to him, but already convinced of his own monstrous nature and convinced that no sane person could ever forgive him for his crimes, Ben Solo went deeper into the darkness, deeper into the persona of Kylo Ren.

Empathy opens us all up to pain and disappointment. I'm under no illusions that seeking to see the best in people who frighten us is without risk. But what I'm calling on you to do is live riskily and with boldness. If we all chose the Bubble-Wrapped existence of stripping our enemies of their humanity, the world we'd live in would be a horror show of violence and upheaval. Like democracy, empathy is hard. The rewards, however, are worth it. Empathy can make you new friends, turn sworn enemies into faithful allies, and break cycles of endless conflict and contempt.

For those least inclined to seek it, the outstretched hand of empathy can bring hope and light the pathway to redemption. The Star Wars saga is a redemption story, only made possible by characters brave enough to live with empathy and all the complications it can create. It's easier to embrace tunnel vision; it's easier to stay busy and breeze past the troubles of your neighbor. In fact, it's very much an act of courage to practice empathy.

And for that reason, we need to talk about fear. How it closes off our minds, hardens our hearts, and limits our sense of possibility. Star Wars is emphatic in its concern about the corrosiveness of fear on its main characters and the societies in which they live, and we should all be taking notes.

Tips: How to Cultivate a Little Empathy

- **"Keep your concentration here and now where it belongs."—Qui-Gon Jinn.** While it's tempting to blame social media for dampening our collective empathy via echo chambers and fake news, the research has shown that even more so, distraction and exhaustion are the real problems.

- **Curb your multitasking.** Being present and focused on one thing at a time allows you more bandwidth to feel for and connect with others you might encounter during your day.

- **Face time matters.** Is your uncle driving you insane on Facebook with his political posts and mean comments? Call him. Go visit. See if the person who angered you online is the same person on the phone with you.

- **Study your own mask.** It can be hard to understand at times, but some people don't want you to see the real them. They hide, cover up, and compensate. Be patient, practice grace, and put yourself in their shoes. Take some time to look in the mirror and review the ways you hide parts of yourself from others. It might help you to be more empathetic when the actions of others confound you.

- **Empathy is a muscle.** You're going to have to work it. That requires seeking out tough conversations and genuinely listening to people with life experiences and pain you don't fully understand.

CHAPTER 3

THE DARK LOVES YOUR GOOD INTENTIONS

"Fear leads to anger, anger leads to hate,
hate leads to suffering."

—Yoda

FEAR

AT THE TIME I'M WRITING THIS, there have been twelve Star Wars feature films, at least four TV series, and announcements of no fewer than seven new Star Wars stories in development by Disney. A lot of things will change with Star Wars over time. Heck, a lot of things already have. But if there's one thing you can be sure of and take to the bank, it's that Star Wars will always be telling stories about both facing fear and the perils of good intentions. In the world we live in, where alarmism and self-righteousness are treated almost as virtues in their own right, nothing could be more valuable for Star Wars to say. Nothing could be more countercultural and rebellious.

Let's be clear—we live in scary times. Terrorism, endless war, school shootings, surging depression among our youth, economic instability, and a viral pandemic just barely behind us that reshaped the world as we once knew it. It's okay to be afraid sometimes, but a Jedi knows there's a cost to letting your fear govern your actions. We're going to be Jedi today. I'm going to tell you now about a few ways in which fear has run amok in our society, in some ways that are out of our hands, and in other ways where we still have the power to reject the seductive lure of fear and aversion to uncertainty.

FEAR HAS TAKEN OVER, BUT WE CAN STILL FIGHT BACK

Long before he fathered Luke Skywalker and Leia, long before he was the dark-cloaked cyborg known as Darth Vader, Anakin Skywalker was just a kind boy raised by a single mother. Making his first appearance in the chronology of Star Wars at age nine in *Episode I: The Phantom Menace* (1999), Anakin is living in slavery on the dusty world of Tatooine when Master Qui-Gon Jinn discovers him. Jinn, sensing his unusual power, offers Anakin the opportunity to leave his mother and his home to train as a Jedi knight. Anakin accepts. As he's preparing to leave with Qui-Gon, it dawns on Anakin that this adventure on which he's about to embark will mean the end of everything he knows and loves. He won't be permitted to go home again by the Jedi. He becomes uncertain. Fearful.

"I don't want things to change," Anakin says to his mother, Shmi Skywalker. "You can't stop the change, any more than you can stop the suns from setting," Shmi answers him. Anakin leaves Tatooine that day to train as a Jedi, but a part of him remains there indefinitely, and he spends the rest of his life besieged by memories of that desert world and tormented by the things left undone there.

There's a reason that the Jedi, this intergalactic order of warrior monks, will only train children. Even a boy of Anakin's age they deem to be too old. It's easy to see why. At nine, Anakin has already formed particularly strong bonds of affection and attachment to his mother and the certain rhythms of life. The Jedi sense this in him from his very first evaluation before the Jedi Council. Yoda posits that Anakin is afraid as he stands before the Jedi, primarily of losing his mother. "What has that got to do with anything?" Anakin responds.

"Everything. Fear is the path to the dark side. Fear leads to anger, anger leads to hate, hate—leads to suffering. I sense much fear in you," says Yoda.

The Jedi were an extraordinarily flawed organization. But they were wholly correct about the danger posed by emotional attachments like those Anakin carried with him into the Jedi Temple. Against their better judgment, the Jedi sanction Anakin's training in hopes that he is indeed the Chosen One, who will bring "balance" to the Force—a feat one could argue he accomplishes. That is, only after Anakin brings about an evil empire that oppresses the galaxy, murders countless innocents, and endures his own period of purgatory within the cold robotic shell of Darth Vader. Fear destroys Anakin Skywalker's life, and it serves as the single most important warning of the Star Wars story.

Control your fear—or it will control you.

What are you afraid of? Probably harm coming to yourself or your loved ones. That's why we buy home security systems. Why do you pay considerable amounts of money for a variety of insurance policies if not for a nagging fear that the unpredictability of this world could land on your doorstep at any time, leaving your family in need or your investments destroyed? In adulthood we call this "being responsible," but it's coming from a *learned* recognition that while things happen that we can't control, we do have some say in how bad the fallout will be. I don't know about you, but I'd never heard of "pet insurance" until adopting my most recent family dog. It was only after he stepped on a massive nail on one of our walks that I felt truly justified in having purchased a pricey policy earlier. Paying that monthly fee for pet insurance offers at least some peace of mind, especially considering the troubles a dog will inevitably get themselves into.

There's a kind of creature out there in the world who knows your every fear, and they are gifted in speaking to your sense of uncertainty. It's not insurance agents, though they are savvy. This creature becomes more powerful the more they stoke your fear. They will even conjure up new things to be afraid of if what has worked in the past stops working. This is, of course, the politician.

As Obi-Wan Kenobi so wisely says, "They are not to be trusted."

There's nothing new about politicians preying on the fears of constituents. But all around us today, fear is warping our private lives and relationship to government in ways that we seldom understand until it's too late. Whether it be confronting foreign terrorism, hateful speech on social media, a deadly pandemic, or the daily challenges of being a parent—fear looms large in our lives.

Before we get to an area where I believe we can actively reject fear and change the culture, I want to start with a place where (I regret to say) we may have failed. But as Master Yoda once said, "The greatest teacher, failure is."

UNDERSTANDING THE "WAR ON TERROR"

Every generation has a defining moment that alters the course of history and leaves an indelible scar on its young people. The COVID-19 pandemic is one such moment. Then there's Pearl Harbor, Vietnam—you know the usual suspects. For me, it was September 11, 2001. I was eleven at the time and sent home from school early to find my mother folding socks in the living room, crying as she watched the horror unfold on TV. I never want to feel like I did that day again.

If you're at all like me, then how you processed 9/11 probably had a big impact on your politics in the years to come. It was my political awakening moment—the reason I started paying attention to the world around me. Something I'm not proud of is how in the years following the attacks, I became quite the foreign policy hawk. Bush was talking about an America that wasn't going to live in fear. He drew a line in the sand, saying, "Every nation, in every region, now has a decision to make.

Either you are with us, or you are with the terrorists."* At the time, that sounded like strength. But as with Anakin Skywalker's challenge to Obi-Wan, "If you're not with me, then you're my enemy," it was anything but.

So we went to war, to stop them over there so we didn't have to face them over here. Twenty years, more than 801,000 lives, and $6.4 trillion dollars later, with active operations in close to eighty countries, I think most Americans understand that this wasn't just a mistake but a form of cognitive dissonance about what it means to not live in fear.[†]

The War on Terror has been an abject failure by its own metrics. In 2003 the Bush administration offered its core objectives for the War on Terror with its stated National Strategy for Combating Terrorism. It read: "The intent of our national strategy is to stop terrorist attacks against the United States, its citizens, its interests, and our friends and allies around the world and ultimately, to create an international environment inhospitable to terrorists and all those who support them."[‡]

If Bush's goal was to reduce the spread and prevalence of terrorism abroad, then the war was an utter failure. According to the Cato Institute, in the seven countries the United States has

---

* "Text: President Bush Addresses the Nation," *Washington Post*, September 20, 2001, https://www.washingtonpost.com/wp-srv/nation/specials/attacked/transcripts/bushaddress_092001.html.

† Brown University, "The cost of the global war on terror: $6.4 trillion and 801,000 lives," November 13, 2019, https://www.brown.edu/news/2019-11-13/costsofwar.

‡ White House, *National Strategy for Combating Terrorism* (White House, 2003), 11; White House, *National Strategy for Counterterrorism* (White House, 2011), 9.

invaded or conducted airstrikes in since 2001, acts of terror rose by an eye-popping 1,900 percent.*

If the goal was to save American lives, well, we've spent more in pursuit of this goal than we lost on 9/11. On that day, 2,996 souls were lost. As of November 2018, just shy of seven thousand US soldiers' lives were taken in Iraq or Afghanistan. If you factor in service member suicides and deaths of despair following combat tours, the situation becomes even more grim.

If the goal was to reassert American power around the world and spread democracy, two things have clearly gone wrong. First, Americans grew undoubtedly war weary and skeptical of Bush-era foreign policy, which in part led to the election of Barack Obama, who promised to walk it all back (which didn't happen). Then came Donald Trump in 2016, pledging to withdraw from these conflicts and challenge our long-standing allies around the globe, whom he cast as "free riders" on American power. To his credit, President Trump reduced troop deployments in a number of countries, but total withdrawal remained elusive during his administration. President Biden, as of July 2021, has committed to an August 31 end to the US military mission in Afghanistan.† A long haul this war has been. Between disrupting US alliances and continuing counterterrorism operations abroad, we only lost

---

* A. Trevor Thrall and Erik Goepner, "Step Back: Lessons for U.S. Foreign Policy from the Failed War on Terror," Cato Institute, June 26, 2017, https://www.cato.org/policy-analysis/step-back-lessons-us-foreign-policy-failed-war-terror.

† "U.S. military mission in Afghanistan will end Aug. 31," Axios, https://www.axios.com/biden-us-afghanistan-withdrawal-taliban-25a62ca3-d49a-40d7-874b-004c20cf04b8.html.

more ground as a global power in the Trump years, the same as during Obama's tenure and Bush's before him. While America has been distracted in the Middle East chasing the ghosts of 9/11, both Russia and China have risen on the world stage in ways that objectively threaten US interests far more than radicalized teenagers building IEDs in Afghanistan.

Second, liberal democracy has receded worldwide in the years since Bush called for a "global democratic revolution" led by the United States. In the Middle East, where the brunt of American military operations has been felt the most, political instability, civil war, and corruption have run rampant. As with Star Wars, if you thought the Empire was bad—wait till you meet the First Order. Iraqis may have been free of Saddam Hussein, a brutal dictator, but within a decade its people endured the rise of ISIS, a theocratic militia with no restraint and a bloodlust the likes of which the modern world had never seen.

Domestically, our own commitments to democratic governance have declined, thanks in no small part to the national security apparatus that popped up in response to 9/11 and the passage of the PATRIOT Act. An American's right to privacy, due process, free speech, and association has declined since 9/11. This isn't an American phenomenon. The swelling of the deep-state intelligence apparatus and shrinking of civil liberties in the name of fighting "terror" have crept into the lives of all the Western democracies that America has historically called its friends.

WHAT STAR WARS UNDERSTOOD
BEFORE WE DID

It was something of a coincidence that the War on Terror and subsequent invasions of Afghanistan and Iraq would happen at the time of George Lucas's prequel trilogy. The fabled creator of Star Wars has long boasted that he knew the backstory of Darth Vader from the earliest years of writing the original Star Wars. Lucas always had a political vision with those original Star Wars films, in which he expressed his misgivings about the Vietnam War era and vaguely hinted about the Nixon administration. The prequels were always bound to follow suit in channeling Lucas's distinctly liberal politics.

But what has always struck me about Episodes I, II, and III is how these movies that were supposedly outlined well before the turn of the century ended up meshing so perfectly with what was unfolding in the news at the time of their release. A threat to the Republic from a frightening new enemy, a congress all too eager to give its head of state a suite of robust emergency powers to meet the threat, and a war predicated on a lie. What Star Wars understood about this situation before the rest of us watched the saga play out on-screen and in reality was that the pursuit of total control by regimes past and present has almost never played out in favor of democratic ideals. This is a theme you can trace back to the original trilogy as well.

Fear, power, self-righteousness, and even good intentions can corrupt and misguide the best of us. And when they do, you lose something along the way that more often than not you can't get back. Maybe it's your liberties, your privacy, a loved one…or a hand. *Reminder: lightsabers are dangerous; use with caution.*

You might recall in *Episode V: The Empire Strikes Back* (1980) Yoda's warning to Luke when he experienced a vision of Han and Leia suffering in Cloud City at the hands of Darth Vader. In a frenzy, Luke cuts short his training on Dagobah and mounts his X-wing to fly to his friends' rescue. Yoda and Obi-Wan are both emphatic that Luke is making a mistake, the same mistake made by his father when he was plagued by similar visions of his wife's untimely death thirty years prior. Yoda tries to stop him, saying, "If you choose the quick and easy path, as Vader did, you will become an agent of evil."

But Luke is convinced Han and Leia will die if he doesn't intervene. I think we can safely say at this point that Luke was wrong. In the end, Leia escapes with the help of a reformed Lando Calrissian, and Han is sealed in carbonite and transported to Jabba the Hutt by Boba Fett—things that had already been set in motion when Luke arrives for his feeble fight against Darth Vader. Luke ultimately goes home short one hand, in need of a new lightsaber, and carrying the burden of knowing Darth Vader to be his father.

It's the low point for Luke on his hero's journey, one that could have been avoided had he not let his actions be governed by fear and uncertainty. This is how the dark side works its will in Star Wars, and it's what George Lucas has challenged fans to reflect on since Star Wars first began and continued on into the Bush years and our "War on Terror."

THAT ROAD TO HELL AND
WHATEVER PAVES IT

You don't wind up with popularly used expressions like "The road to hell is paved with good intentions" without there being some merit or abiding understanding in the wisdom of such a proverb. "Facilis descensus Averno," reads Virgil's *Aeneid*, dating back to roughly 25 BC—"The descent to hell is easy." You're likely familiar with this notion and have heard it before. Star Wars is one of our epoch's most effective funnels for timeless philosophy and spirituality such as this. Characters like Yoda hold inside them all the greats: the Stoics, Buddha, Confucius, Christ (just to name a few)...and as such, Star Wars aligns nicely with those powerful few words from Virgil. Remember when Luke Skywalker asks Yoda on Dagobah if the dark side is more powerful? Yoda replies, "No. Quicker, easier, more seductive."

This is something most people understand to be true. The American founders surely did. That's why the idea is baked into American government that so much of governing is somewhat slow and arduous and requires frustrating levels of consensus between political factions and warring branches (legislative, judicial, and executive). As politics becomes more mired in gridlock, indecision, and disagreeableness, naturally you hear a lot of "we must do *something*" proposed in opposition to process and coolheadedness.

But let's face it: being "cool as a cucumber" is not politically popular.

Taking action, doing something—anything! Now *that* is popular. *Action* is the clarion call of politicians and fearful constituents. It's the call of the loving parent who watches on TV as news of a school shooting unfolds just a few counties over. The sad reality is that most of us don't have to imagine such a thing, considering national traumas like the massacres at Columbine, Sandy Hook Elementary, and Marjory Stoneman Douglas High are etched into our memories for life. There will never be a day when I drop my own daughter off at school without experiencing flashes of pain in the form of CNN news headlines saying, "Yet another school shooting." Now, consider what might happen if you or I were to sit down in front of Master Yoda at the Jedi Temple on Coruscant and ask, "Master Yoda, I'm plagued by visions of pain, suffering, and death regarding my children. I'm afraid of harm that could befall them at school. What must I do?" There's a good chance Yoda might respond similarly to the way he does regarding Anakin Skywalker's visions of personal loss: "The fear of loss is a path to the dark side. Death is a natural part of life. Rejoice for those around you who transform into the Force. Mourn them, do not. Miss them, do not. Attachment leads to jealousy. The shadow of greed, that is."

Conservative author and public speaker Arthur Brooks has spoken a great deal about his appreciation for Buddhism and his meetings with Tibetan monks, including the Dalai Lama. On his podcast, *The Art of Happiness*, Brooks described asking one of the monks how to better understand bad feelings, such as anger, fear, or disgust. He recalls the response: "You see them as a signal that you have an attachment that you need to address."* Remember what I said about Yoda being a funnel for real-world philosophy and spirituality?

Because I am an imperfect person, I for one would be agitated—maybe even furious at either response. Anakin appeared low-key livid at it himself. *You mean to tell me that my problem is not the mortal danger looming over my loved ones but that I am too attached to them?* Bogus. No half-decent parent, sibling, spouse, or friend can think this way. Sure, Anakin wasn't supposed to have a spouse for exactly this reason while living his life as a Jedi. But I haven't signed up to be a Jedi, and (probably) neither have you.

So what are we supposed to do? Yoda says to Anakin, "Train yourself to let go of everything you fear to lose." Should we embrace this kind of dispassionate zen as parents, as husbands and wives, and as citizens? Probably not. We aren't a society of monks. We should love big, but perhaps we should be willing to hold the reins more loosely.

I told you that certain battles with fear, like that of the War on Terror, may well be out of our hands at this point. There's a saying that goes something like, "What freedoms you give up to the government, you won't likely get back," and in this case,

---

* Arthur Brooks, *The Art of Happiness* (podcast), March 15, 2021, https://arthurbrooks .com/podcast/overcoming-a-fear-of-failure/.

that rings true to me. But one battle lost isn't game over. There are other areas much closer to our daily lives, much more within our reach, where we can reject living in a fearful society. We can still change the culture.

CLEARING YOUR MIND OF FEAR ISN'T JUST HARD—IT'S UNNATURAL

One of things I've noticed in my own life since becoming a parent is that getting a playdate is not as easy as it was when I was growing up. And that was before the global pandemic and the added wrinkles of COVID-19 in getting your kid out of the house for a few hours. People today are not just very busy, but they're also very guarded. I'll never forget the icy text I received from a neighbor after I allowed my daughter to go knock on their door to see if their kids would like to come outside and play. For something as simple as playtime for their kids, modern people expect coordination and thorough familiarity with their children's playmates as well as their parents.

In 2017 I went to an event in New Hampshire put on by the Free State Project, this libertarian affair where families and individuals camp out in the countryside of New Hampshire for a few days. There are some coordinated events like dance parties, policy panels, and live podcast tapings you can sit in on, but a good deal of the fun is unorganized and somewhat spontaneous. It was there I learned about "free-range parenting," a concept I was familiar with from my own childhood and the movies but didn't know the name for. Put simply, it's just the now dated idea that kids could hop on their bikes and go roam the community with their friends as long as they were home for dinner. It's the kind of childhoods you see brought to life in old movies like *E.T.* (1982) and *The Goonies* (1985), or, more recently, in *Stranger Things* on Netflix.

Kids were running around this handful of acres in New Hampshire like a pack of wolves, mostly unaccompanied by adults and doing their own thing, while their parents did theirs. It's weird to me how unfamiliar and uncomfortable this felt to me when I saw it.

At the core of this now countercultural parenting philosophy are two principles: that kids have always been and still are remarkably capable little creatures and that parents shouldn't face government sanction for choosing to let their kids have space to learn in this way. But in recent history, a new kind of parenting has gone mainstream, and it's crowded out space for more hands-off parents to let their kids enjoy some freedom. "Helicopter parenting," as it's often referred to, is the more contemporary and familiar spin on raising kids, and it's the one I encounter every day, as I described, when trying to get my own child to go outside and play with her neighbors and classmates. It's frustrating.

Let Grow, a nonprofit dedicated to educating and offering resources to families interested in free-range parenting and also protecting themselves from legal inquisitions by the likes of Child Protective Services, says people today are "bubble-wrapping" their kids because of "the twin fears" that "either their kids will be snatched by a demonic clown...or they won't get into Harvard."*

I worry about those demonic clowns, as someone born in 1989, which was the peak of serial killings in the United States. I've watched news coverage on the worst of the worst stories, and you have too. Child kidnappings. Assault. Murder. It's the stuff of nightmares, and when these stories have fully sunken their claws into your psyche, every unfamiliar face on the street gradually looks more and more like a threat to your child, instead of just a passerby, which they more than likely are.

At play here is the same dark force that tainted our national response to terrorism after 9/11, which is a sensationalism around worst-case scenarios. The news media is in part to blame for this, but the news media is just as much a reflection of what we want as consumers as it is a driver of our behaviors out in the world. If feel-good realism drove clicks and kept eyeballs glued to TV screens, well, then, CNN, Fox News, and the rest of the media would churn out content reminding us how exceedingly rare it is to die in a terror attack, or how freakishly uncommon a kidnapping really is. No one wants to hear that crime in America is at its all-time lowest point in decades or be lectured about how serial killers were more a blip on the timeline for criminality than a still-looming threat in our communities.

---

* Let Grow, "Let Grow Looks at Common Child Safety Myths and Facts," https://letgrow.org/child-safety-myth-busting/.

But as a species we are drawn to our darkest visions of what could be, and that's helped humanity to survive and thrive as long as it has. We don't want to go the way of the dodo, which has been extinct for over three hundred years. So we make trade-offs, like between our freedoms and our safety. The trouble is recognizing when our fear is clouding our ability to see and act reasonably.

Luke continued his questioning of Yoda about the dark side, and asked, "How am I to know the good side from the bad?" To which Yoda responded, "You will know...when you are calm, at peace, passive." We call this reason, or logic—and it's exceedingly hard. Lived experience and the scars we may carry inform our decisions much more than cold statistical thinking.

THE DOOM LOOP OF APOCALYPTIC THINKING

We should give Anakin a little bit of grace for how badly he handles the events of *Episode III: Revenge of the Sith* (2005). When he begins to wake in a fright from dreams of his wife, Padmé, dying in childbirth, it's not as if he's never experienced such visions before. In *Episode II: Attack of the Clones* (2002), he experienced premonitions linked to his mother on Tatooine, whom he'd left behind ten years prior so that he could to become a Jedi, and, in that case, the visions came true. Shmi Skywalker truly was being held captive, starved and tortured by Tatooine's indigenous peoples, the Tusken Raiders. Anakin took action, but arrived too late. His mother died in his arms, broken and destitute.

Anger exploded into hatred within Anakin, and in response, he murdered the entire village of raiders—the men, the women, and the children too. These sorts of things a Jedi doesn't likely come back from, as was the case for Anakin Skywalker in his march toward becoming the infamous Darth Vader.

Remember: *fear* ⟶ *anger* ⟶ *hate* ⟶ *suffering.*

What I've always wondered about Anakin's visions is how much they are generated by his own personal anxiety and how much they are the dark side of the Force actively preying on his vulnerability. Either way, Anakin's angst over visions of Padmé's eventual death is what you'd call a self-fulfilling prophecy. Envisioning Padmé suffering and appearing to die in childbirth, Anakin sets out to find the power to save her life, which leads him straight into the arms of Palpatine (a Sith lord), who's eager to tempt him with the promise of knowledge that could prevent the worst from happening. As in the Christian Bible's description of the fall of man within the Garden of Eden, a serpent promises enlightenment and, by extension, power. Palpatine is no different.

After Anakin essentially sells his soul to the devil and carries out the wholesale slaughter of the Jedi Order, he tries to get Padmé to sanction what he's done in her name. It breaks her heart, and Anakin becomes violent in response, which presumably is what complicates her pregnancy and leads to her death as she delivers their twins, Luke and Leia.

Not once had Anakin considered that he could be the cause of his own worst nightmares, that his inability to let go, as Yoda advised, was yielding exactly the kind of bad outcomes he so desperately wanted to avoid.

It's exactly this kind of irony that brings me back to the conundrum of modern parenting. Kids are either being kept at home more and dwelling online in the comfort of their bedrooms, or they've been given cell phones for the express purpose of their parents being able to keep tabs on them. No one seemed to question this entire premise until after a majority of kids were in possession of their own smartphones by age eleven. Prior to 2015, kids weren't getting phones, even the more rudimentary flip phones, until about age fourteen*.

Sure, smartphones are an awesome technology, and they've made monitoring your kids' whereabouts (protecting them) all the easier, but this technology has also brought with it unprecedented exposure to things like pornography, gruesome online violence, and relentless cyberbullying from classmates. Bullying used to be a kind of torment that at least ended when the school bell rang—now it can follow kids wherever they go. There's no getting away from the fact that mental illness, depression, and anxiety-based disorders are spreading like wildfire among younger generations.

I want to take my own advice here and not be overly sensational about the negative effects of social media and technology on kids, as *all things* can be negative in excess. But I want to point

---

* Anya Kamenetz, "It's A Smartphone Life: More Than Half Of U.S. Children Now Have One," NPR, October 31, 2019, https://www.npr.org/2019/10/31/774838891/its-a-smartphone-life-more-than-half-of-u-s-children-now-have-one.

to a societal failure of good intentions that we've not properly litigated in the public square. Are young kids really better off at home and online versus roaming their communities and getting into a little trouble with their friends? I don't believe so, and yet we've undoubtedly restructured our society around the former.

Why is it that a parent in Maryland can be brought to court and even have their children taken away from them by the state for allowing them to walk unaccompanied in their neighborhood*, but no one is questioning parents' capability or penchant for negligence when they get their six-year-old an iPhone and allow them to have a TikTok account? The state of Utah had to pass an entire "free-range parenting" law in 2018 to shield parents from legal action if their kids were found to be roaming freely, as was once considered completely normal circa 1990. It doesn't make a whole lot of sense that such a law even had to be enacted, and it speaks to a larger problem of fear ruling our lives today—far more than reason.

When fear governs our thinking, we find ourselves in a sort of doom loop, hurtling from one apocalyptic scenario to the next, in many cases generating new anxieties and new fears within ourselves, simply so we can have something that's motivating us toward action. This can serve us well in some cases, and very poorly in others.

---

* Donna St. George, "Parents investigated for neglect after letting kids walk home alone," *Washington Post*, January 14, 2015, https://www.washingtonpost.com/local/education/maryland-couple-want-free-range-kids-but-not-all-do/2015/01/14/d406c0be-9c0f-11e4-bcfb-059ec7a93ddc_story.html.

FEAR AND THE DELICATE DANCE WITH HOPE

I pointed to some areas in which fear has generally been good for humankind. Fear is why we get insurance policies and mind the speed limit (usually) when driving. Fear is one of the reasons we live indoors. At some point, our ancestors must have gotten fed up with being preyed on by wolves and saber-toothed tigers and decided some walls and doors might be in order.

Fear can give us momentum and shake us out of our complacency. If approached with some sense of humility and curiosity, fear can yield something beautiful in our lives: hope.

It's what Princess Leia is always talking about in the face of certain doom. At the rousing end of *Rogue One: A Star Wars Story* (2016), the rebels hand Leia the Death Star plans after narrowly escaping slaughter at the hands of Darth Vader. They ask Leia what it is they just risked life and limb for, and "hope" is what she tells them. Roll credits! She's right: the Death Star plans offer a glimmer of hope to a fledgling rebellion aiming to deliver a first real blow to the Empire, but it's also a death sentence. The Empire will stop at nothing to get the plans back, going so far as to annihilate Leia's entire planet in response. Two billion Alderaanians murdered. Is it worth it? Given the Empire's penchant for indiscriminate violence and its possession of weapons of mass destruction, yes, it is.

Star Wars is a world of extremes, whereas many of the choices we make in our own lives are more or less boring. If I decide to change jobs or to strike out on my own and start a business, that's scary, but it's not "make the Death Star trench run" scary.

Nevertheless, we do these things because we have dreams or ambitions, and because there's a visible light (or cleverly placed exhaust port) at the end of that scary trench, beckoning you toward it with the opportunity for a better life. This is how fear can make us better. But only if we're willing to rise, name, and confront it.

CONFRONTING FEAR IS THE
DESTINY OF A JEDI

Award-winning writer and mindfulness coach Elisa Boxer wrote once that when working on mindfulness with her students, she asks them to acknowledge fear whenever it washes over them.* The idea is to name it. At the time I'm writing this, I'm stepping away from salaried work for the first time in my professional life to start my own consulting and media business, as well as write my first book. Naming my fear in this instance is quite easy. I'm afraid of failing—of disappointing my wife and daughter, and of the shame I'll feel if this venture doesn't work out.

But fear masquerades at times as deliberation. You'll find yourself extra tired and glued to your bed in the morning, telling yourself you have a lot to think about regarding some big decision or deadlines in your work. More often than not, no

---

* Elisa Boxer, "This 2 Step Process Can Move You Out of Fear and Into Action," Inc., December 13, 2017, https://www.inc.com/elisa-boxer/heres-how-to-conquer-your-fear-according-to-science-and-yoda.html.

such deliberation is taking place. You're hiding and afraid to face the fear for whatever reason.

This is natural. There's a reason I started this exploration of fear with a look at the irrational culture of anxiety, control, and uncertainty that guides our politics and even parenting. It relates really well to what pushed Anakin down the dark path from which there's no return. Anakin didn't get a lot of great advice, both because his problems were kept a secret from the Jedi and because the Jedi's doctrine left little room for the kind of help he really needed. But there is sound and direct advice to be found in Star Wars about fear, and it's actually in the same scene where Anakin goes to Yoda for help with his nightmares. In the novelization of *Revenge of the Sith*, Yoda also says to him, "Named must your fear before banish it you can."

If Anakin had tried to name his fear, it's possible his own self-ishness could have been revealed to him. His fear wasn't harm befalling Padmé or his unborn children; it was just that things were outside of his control—something that had bothered him since his earliest days on Tatooine, growing up with no power of self-determination.

Perhaps some of the most powerful, simple, timeless, and true words in the Star Wars saga come from Luke Skywalker, when the departed Jedi Master confronts Rey as she wallows in despair on his island in the final act of *Episode IX: The Rise of Skywalker* (2019): "Confronting fear is the destiny of a Jedi." Fear had over-whelmed Rey, fear of who she really is, and by extension, what she could become. Luke faced a similar reckoning following

Darth Vader's famous reveal of their familial connection, and it's the kind of thing that will either propel heroes forward or bring them grinding to a halt.

Fear is like that. I've alluded to the fact that fear is part of being human, and in the long arc of our history it's reasonable fear that has helped us survive. But it's determining what's reasonable that is so difficult.

If you struggle with this, you're certainly not alone. Studies have shown for a long time that Americans are lousy at assessing their own risk and exposure to danger. Between 1994 and 2004, the national Survey of Economic Expectations asked respondents to put a number on their percent likelihood of being robbed on the street.* For that decade, it came out that 15 percent of those surveyed thought it was likely they'd be robbed. The actual level of risk? A mere 1.2 percent. Now, we can be gracious in some contexts, such as conceding that in this time period (the 1990s) the country was experiencing a crime wave in major cities that garnered a great deal of media excitement and subsequent public anxiety. The problem is that if you zoom out, the '90s were still just a blip on the radar in what's been a massive decrease in crime in the United States over time. Between 1993 and 2018, the rate of violent crimes per thousand Americans (age twelve and older) plummeted from eighty in 1993 to

---

* Maggie Koerth and Amelia Thomson-DeVeaux, "Many Americans Are Convinced Crime Is Rising In The U.S. They're Wrong," FiveThirtyEight, April 3, 2020, https://fivethirtyeight.com/features/many-americans-are-convinced-crime-is-rising-in-the-u-s-theyre-wrong/.

just twenty-three, says the Bureau of Justice Statistics.* Politicians, though, don't talk about stuff like this. In fact, both sides actively downplay the facts of risk and relative danger anytime it advances their agenda.

In America, the odds you'll be killed by an animal are one in 1,489,177—the odds of being killed in an attack hatched by foreign-born terrorists? One in 3,710,897. Native-born terrorists? One in 27,482,415.† The way progressives talk today, you'd think homegrown neo-Nazi extremists are hatching attacks on every street corner. Conservatives continue to talk about refugees from abroad like they're all in cahoots with al-Qaeda, and yet you still have a higher-percentage chance of dying at the hands of your own clothes than by those of a terrorist mixed in among refugees. By the tail end of the COVID-19 pandemic, it became clear that the risk of hospitalization for children by the virus was less than 1 percent. Yet we still allowed schools and summer camps to close and stop serving those most in need of their services.

You hear these kinds of statistics all the time, but they bear repeating because we need to have this kind of perspective when grappling with fear and uncertainty. When we fail to keep things in perspective, we get the "War on Terror," limitless surveillance,

---

* Rachel E. Morgan, Ph.D., and Barbara A. Oudekerk, Ph.D, "Criminal Victimization, 2018," U.S. Department of Justice, September 2019, https://bjs.ojp.gov/content/pub/pdf/cv18.pdf.

† Alex Nowrasteh, "More Americans Die in Animal Attacks than in Terrorist Attacks," Cato Institute, March 8, 2018, https://www.cato.org/blog/more-americans-die-animal-attacks-terrorist-attacks.

and the surrender of our rights, all imposed by politicians who trade in fear like commodities. You get gyms with caution tape closing off access to water fountains during COVID, even though the science had evolved and shown surface transmission wasn't a meaningful threat to public health.

Depending on where you live, you may not even have the established right to send your child around the corner to pick up milk from the store without serious legal repercussions. Most people don't want to live in a society where the government can read your emails on a whim or take your kids away from you for letting them out of your sight, but it's the society we're building.

Anakin Skywalker became Darth Vader because his fears and inability to live with uncertainty took up an unreasonable amount of real estate in his mind. Letting go or living with it were not options as far as he was concerned. We must all take the lesson of his fall seriously, because it meant not only his own lifetime of suffering, but also the subjugation of everyone around him. This can happen to any of us when the anxieties associated with parenting, marriage, governing, and civic participation begin to outweigh our capacity for reason.

Fear shrinks our world instead of opening it up to new possibilities. Far from being something we can explain away as merely self-preservation, fear takes such a strong hold of people that it prevents them from making changes that could improve or even save their lives.

This brings me to another key principle of Star Wars that runs throughout its films: redemption. Numerous Star Wars characters experience redemption in one way or another, but most of all it's the villains who are redeemed. What you find in the stories of Anakin Skywalker (Darth Vader) and of his grandson, Ben Solo (Kylo Ren), is that fear presents a significant obstacle to their coming back to the light and into the arms of family. Fear interacts with shame and doubt in such a way that it closes the door in our minds to self-improvement and change. Fear smothers hope.

The entire world needs to rediscover an appreciation for redemption, and as individuals we have to confront the fact that while cultural rot such as "cancel culture" poses a real threat to redemptive stories and personal growth, often the only thing in our way is ourselves. Next we're going to look at where "hope" fits into the Star Wars narrative, and how a little bit more of it could help fix our world.

Tips: You Can Subdue Your
Fear—Here's How to Start

- **Name your fear.** Don't let it loom in your mind as a shape-shifting phantom. When you speak honestly, and with a bit of vulnerability, the true shape of your fear may start to become clear.

- **Learn to let go.** You've heard the phrase "Hold on loosely," and you've probably heard the saying "Let go and let God." The sooner we admit our inability to control every facet of our lives and the world around us, the sooner we can know peace.

- **Be prepared.** Remind yourself daily to discern what you can control and that which you cannot. My internet crashed a ton in 2020 while working from home during the pandemic, and I was often fearful of missing a meeting or being dropped from an important call. So I made backup plans. That lowered my constantly simmering anxiety a great deal.

- **Be aware that your fear is a commodity for the powerful.** The media, politicians, and corporations study your anxieties and pander to them to accumulate power and sell you stuff. That doesn't mean be reckless, that doesn't mean be irresponsible, but don't be a sucker.

- **Consider evidence.** Statistics and risk analysis won't wipe away your fears, but they ease some of the terror you may feel about the unknown.

CHAPTER 4

WHAT REBELLIONS ARE BUILT ON

"Hope is like the sun. If you only believe in it when you see it, you'll never make it through the night."

—General Leia Organa

HOPE

THIS IS NEVER GOING TO END," my daughter cried just a few days before Christmas of 2020. Her head rested on my shoulder, and I could feel her tears starting to seep through my shirt. This went on for some time, all because I had the bright idea of asking her if she was excited about the coming new year. She was not. I couldn't blame her.

I've never experienced something like the coronavirus pandemic in my life. What Bill Gates called a "once-in-a-century pathogen" in February 2020* shaped up to be exactly that by year's end—a seismic force that changed the world as we knew it. In the week between Christmas and New Year's Eve 2020, the US death toll surpassed 330,000, with roughly 1.75 million dead

---

* Noah Higgins-Dunn, "Bill Gates: Coronavirus may be 'once-in-a-century pathogen we've been worried about,'" CNBC, February 18, 2020, https://www.cnbc.com/2020/02/28/bill-gates-says-coronavirus-may-be-once-in-a-century-pathogen.html.

worldwide. No industry or sector of the economy was immune from the effects of the virus and subsequent government actions (and overreactions) to slow its spread. Millions of jobs were lost. Small businesses everywhere closed their doors in the first wave of government-imposed lockdowns, only to never reopen after modest assistance was given by Congress in the form of direct cash aid and business loans. Schools closed, forcing children across America into "distance learning" and classes via Zoom, a worthy experiment but one that proved disastrous for educational outcomes and the mental health of children, parents, and teachers.

When did you first feel hopeless in 2020? I have yet to speak with someone who survived that no-good, awful year who said they never felt a moment of weakness, despair, or hopelessness about the pandemic. And I want to emphasize "survived," because it hit close to home for over half of Americans. Pew Research found that 54 percent of Americans knew someone who'd been hospitalized or died from COVID-19.* For me it was in the first week of November that I felt the stabbing pain of hopelessness. A line was wrapping around my local Costco, with people loading up on paper products and sanitizer as fears of a second COVID wave were crystallizing alongside anxieties regarding the presidential election. It felt for a time as if this was

---

* Cary Funk and Alec Tyson, "Intent to Get a COVID-19 Vaccine Rises to 60% as Confidence in Research and Development Process Increases," Pew Research Center, December 3, 2020, https://www.pewresearch.org/science/2020/12/03/intent-to-get-a-covid-19-vaccine-rises-to-60-as-confidence-in-research-and-development-process-increases/.

really it; this was going to be life from now on. Masking up. Social distancing. Elbow bumps instead of handshakes. Polite nods instead of warm hugs.

With this crying child on me, and my mind racing to find "perfect Dad-like wisdom" to try to lift her up from this moment of despair, I began to cycle through the pop-culture encyclopedia in my brain for something to say to her. Because let's be honest: there's nothing I could say to her that she could count on. Our governor could reimpose lockdowns and business closures the next day on a whim, and Dr. Anthony Fauci could change his mind again about the merit of reopening schools.

"Do you have hope?" I asked her.

"Yeah, but..."

I continued, "Hope is like the sun. If you only believe in it when you see it, you'll never make it through the night."

She paused and closed her eyes, letting one more tear slide down her cheek as she thought it over. She knew the line. My nicely timed Star Wars reference was to a quote delivered by Vice Admiral Holdo in *Episode VIII: The Last Jedi* (2017). Holdo, a towering, proud, wiry-framed woman with purple hair, offered this wisdom to the brash "flyboy" Poe Dameron to try to assuage his doubts about how the Resistance would escape the First Order, whose Star Destroyers and legion of stormtroopers were bearing down on them. The situation was what you might call...well, hopeless. Holdo and Dameron both held these words in high regard, because they were those of Princess Leia, or General Organa as she's known at this point in her career.

Hope really *is* like the sun. It warms us, it guides us, and it helps to fill our worlds with color. But the sun can also become lost behind clouds and shrouded in impossible darkness, with no clear end in sight to that gray haze. If you don't know that the sun is in fact there, or believe that it will eventually emerge from those clouds, you really will struggle to make it to that next warm day.

We need hope. In this chapter you're going to learn about why hope matters, how you can cultivate it, and what to do when hope feels out of your reach. No matter where you stand in your politics, left or right, you might notice there are always forces calling you toward either your better angels or your most base impulses. Are your leaders offering you hope and inspiring you? Or are they selling cynicism, fear, and doubt?

When it comes to social movements, including revolutions (or rebellions), hope is the ingredient that so often can make or break them. We're going to look at some movements driving conversation in the United States and determine if they're driven by hope.

Like the Rebel Alliance, which faced down the impossibly powerful Empire, we, too, have a choice to make in how we talk about and shape the future. Will we be a people who wallow in despair and nihilism, gratifying our primal urges as the world falls apart...or will we do the hard work of building the kind of world we want to see?

LEIA'S IMPOSSIBLE HOPE

Grand Moff Wilhuff Tarkin was never going to spare Alderaan. When Princess Leia misled him about the location of the rebel base in *Episode IV: A New Hope* (1977), naming the mostly desolate world of Dantooine as the location of the base, Tarkin had already planned a murderous demonstration of the Death Star's power for all the galaxy to see. Alderaan was Leia's home. Her parents and fellow rebels, Bail and Breha Organa, were on the planet at the time Tarkin gave the order for the massive orbital space station to fire on the planet. Millions upon millions of lives were snuffed out in an instant. The Death Star, which the Rebellion had risked everything to stop, was now fully operational. Tarkin, whose belief in the Death Star was rooted in the cynical goal of solidifying the Empire's hold on power through absolute fear, had made his move and put all his chips on that belief.

He was wrong. I've always marveled watching *A New Hope* and taking note of the poise and resoluteness of Princess Leia throughout that original Star Wars film. While Luke Skywalker is a beacon of hope to audiences in his own way, Leia strikes me as unique. After escaping the Death Star with Luke, Han Solo, and Chewbacca, it's Leia who comforts Luke for his loss of Obi-Wan Kenobi. He looks shattered. Leia, on the other hand, having just lost everything in the most literal sense, remains as motivated as ever. She has the eye of the tiger from start to finish.

How the heck does she do it?

WHAT OUR FUTURE VISION
SAYS ABOUT US

We've been living through some seriously dark days for mankind. Between repeated economic downturns and a global pandemic the likes of which haven't been seen since the Spanish Flu of 1918, things have felt pretty darn awful. Millions have died worldwide from the coronavirus, and, as noted above, if you were in the United States you had a fifty-fifty chance of personally knowing someone hospitalized or killed by the virus. It's not a surprise that mental health professionals are seeing an unprecedented spike in anxiety, depression, and suicides across multiple age groups and demographics. Political systems were already straining before the pandemic even began. Populist movements and authoritarian leaders have risen across the globe and chipped away at the democratic consensus that has defined the post–World War II order. In the United States, political violence has flared to levels not seen since the tumultuous 1960s.

In 2020 we saw a summer of protests spurred on by racially tinged instances of police brutality, protests that quickly spiraled into weeks of major cities burning, businesses being looted, and street violence of all sorts. Progressive groups like Black Lives Matter and the black-clad militants of Antifa defined much of the media discussion and debates held around dinner tables in those dramatic months. That is, until the incident of January 6, 2021, when Far-Right demonstrators gathered in Washington, DC, to protest the counting and certification of Electoral

College votes for Joe Biden. At the behest of President Donald Trump, the crowd morphed into a mob and descended on Congress, breaking into the Capitol and ransacking the closest thing we have to a sanctuary for democracy. The business of government was halted only for a few hours, the votes were counted and certified, but by the end at least four people were dead, including one Capitol police officer. Donald Trump became the first president to ever be impeached more than once by Congress as a result of what happened.

Something is changing. Storm clouds are gathering.

I don't know about you, but I did not have a pandemic, nationwide riots, and an attack on Congress written on my 2020 Bingo card. This isn't the future I dreamed of. Maybe you grew up believing mankind would be in space by now, living like *The Jetsons* or even blasting through hyperspace like Han Solo aboard the Millennium Falcon to new and exciting worlds. It can be kind of demoralizing. We thought we'd have flying cars, but instead, all we got was curbside pickup at Starbucks.

It's easy to forget that things are getting better all around us in ways that are hard to see. Since the time of my birth in 1989, income per person in the United States has risen 67 percent, life expectancy is up 4 percent, and food supply has increased by 7 percent.* When my father was just a boy, mankind was putting its feet on the moon for the first time; today we're making huge

---

* HumanProgress.org, "Explore how much the world has changed since you were born," https://www.humanprogress.org/ylin/?the-comparison-country=264&the-country =167&the-year=1989.

strides toward manned missions to Mars. Heck, the robotic rovers we've sent to Mars in recent years have uncovered proof that there used to be water on that distant red planet. Once the question was, Is there life out there in the stars? Now we've moved on to a new question—*Where* is that life?

You know that scene in *Episode IV: A New Hope* (1977), with Luke Skywalker standing in the desert at dusk, watching the twin suns of Tatooine set on the horizon? It's one of the most enduring moments of Star Wars from generation to generation. The lonely dreamer looking out on the world and believing there must be more to it than what they can see. Luke is all of us at that moment. It doesn't matter if you're Elon Musk, risking a fortune on a new space shuttle to make it to Mars, or if you're a young girl living in a cramped Chicago apartment with five siblings and dreaming of making it big in Hollywood…lifting your family out of poverty in the process.

Maybe you call this hope. Maybe you call it the American Dream. These things go hand in hand. Do *you* have hope?

HOPE BEYOND HOPE

"Hope" is a lot of things. In our minds it can be personified, objectified, or embodied in places, faith, and prose. But it does have a definition. *Merriam-Webster's Dictionary* defines hope as "to cherish a desire with anticipation: to want something to happen" or as "desire accompanied by expectation of or belief in fulfillment."

In short, it's to want something you can have, at least in

theory. I want very badly to have the Jedi power of levitating objects and moving them around my house with my mind, but I don't have hope of achieving such a thing, nor should I. It's not within the realm of possibility. But what if I watched enough YouTube videos made by weirdos living in their mothers' basements, telling me beyond a shadow of a doubt that I'm wrong, and this power is in fact attainable? All I'd have to do, according to these armchair wizards of the web, is watch enough of their videos and wire them some money. There's a good chance that at some point you'll become bitter and angry. After all, someone sold you false goods, hope beyond hope.

This is what happens to Anakin Skywalker when he is told by a supposed friend, Chancellor Palpatine, about the power to control life and death that is known only to the Sith. Anakin, suffering from visions of his wife dying in childbirth, is lured in by a twisted kind of hope we might understand as an intergalactic spin on the trope of the snake-oil salesman who travels from town to town hawking miracle cures that almost certainly will let the buyer down.

Just as hope can push the likes of Princess Leia forward through a tragedy like the destruction of Alderaan, hope can also move a desperate and loving husband to spend the last of his savings or sell the house to get that cure from the roving snake-oil salesman. There is a light and dark side to everything.

In the Christian tradition, hope sits alongside faith and charity as one of the core virtues and guiding lights of the religion. The notion that God would send his son to mankind in order to deliver them from sin and, by extension, damnation is a significant dose of hope for a people in need of redemption. Absent that guiding light and the possibility of salvation, you'd have masses of people mired in endless cycles of guilt and despair.

Hope here is more than a feeling. It's not something that washes over you and leaves like an emotion (i.e., anger, fear, sadness). No. As a virtue, it's something you discover and hold on to for dear life, despite everything the world will throw at you. Hope is the life vest. Hope is the parachute when you've jumped out of a plane. It's like faith. You can become a person who is hopeful (and positive), or you can become cynical, someone who is predisposed to see the worst in people and in the future.

Even worse, absent hope you can devolve into a thing called nihilism, a particularly toxic kind of hopelessness rooted in the belief that nothing matters. Most people aren't born this way. It's a learned behavior and one increasingly popular with young people and lauded throughout our popular and political culture.

Throughout Star Wars, audiences understand rightly that the Empire is an incredibly evil and morally bankrupt regime. With this being crystal clear, would-be rebels have a choice to make in how they make their stand against the Empire. It's not good enough to simply oppose the Empire. To win, the Rebel Alliance has to do three things: First, let the people of the galaxy know they're not alone in feeling angry about the state of things. Second, let people know that the Empire can actually be beaten. Third, paint a picture of a better future.

The Rebel Alliance does all of these things. In our own world, the majority of successful movements and political campaigns do so as well.

HOPE ON THE BALLOT

Many of the crossroads we come to in our lives are choices not between going left or right, but more so moving forward or moving backward. In some cases, there's also the option to stand still. The first election I voted in was 2008, the contest between US senators Barack Obama and John McCain. The narrative around that choice was made pretty clear by the campaigns they ran and the slogans they leaned on. McCain's was "Reform, Prosperity, Peace." At least to me as a then college Republican, it was a campaign about staying the course—standing still. We all know what Barack Obama's campaign was about: "Hope and Change." Obama carried the election easily by 365 to 173 electoral votes and nearly ten million in the popular vote.* America chose this thing called "hope" over what was seen as a continuation of the Bush years, both on foreign policy and the economy, which had sunk into recession months prior to the election.

Believe or not, the 2016 election was similar in one key way. Donald Trump ran on "Make America Great Again," and Hillary Clinton with "Stronger Together." Which one was about changing the status quo and offering a vision of what could be?

---

* 2008 Electoral College Results, National Archives, https://www.archives.gov/electoral -college/2008.

It was MAGA. Sure, Trump was harkening to the past in a way, but he did so to point in a direction that America should actively go. His message resonated in the states where it mattered most, and Donald Trump became president. Fast-forward to 2020, and it came as no surprise to me that Trump lost his bid for reelection. "Keep America Great" was the status quo message of the campaign and couldn't have been more poorly timed, given the devastating impact of the COVID-19 pandemic. People weren't feeling like things were so great. Biden had a slew of slogans, "Build Back Better" being the most frequently used of them. In that election, he was pointing to new things, not just rebuilding a country ravaged by the coronavirus, but making it better than ever before. Vague, but compelling.

The start of 2021 was more or less the immediate sequel to the prior November election that saw Donald Trump relegated to one term and Joe Biden and Kamala Harris ascending to the White House. The US Senate races in Georgia had been sent to a January 5 runoff between Democrats Raphael Warnock and Jon Ossoff and Republicans Kelly Loeffler and David Perdue. If the Democrats managed to win both Georgia seats, they'd win control of the Senate and officially make Majority Leader Mitch McConnell the minority leader, and give President-Elect Joe Biden a unified Democratic government. It's not that the Democrats had a particularly hope-based message, but more so that the Republican campaign in Georgia had devolved into total cynicism bordering on nihilistic self-destruction.

You have to wonder how the Republican National Committee

felt about the head of the party, Donald Trump, tweeting through-out the week of the Georgia runoff that the election he'd just lost was "rigged" and "stolen." Worse still, ballot machines became the primary target of the president's Twitter rage, which he maligned as being tampered with by Dominion Voting Systems, the com-pany that made the machines. If you were a Georgia Republican working two full-time jobs and barely making ends meet, would you feel particularly compelled to go back out to vote a second time in January if you were convinced the process was rigged anyway? It couldn't have helped. Demographic change in Geor-gia, combined with slightly suppressed Republican turnout for the runoff, led to a Democratic victory for both seats.

As we start to unpack the dualism between hope and nihil-ism, I want you to keep that example in mind. Because while you could be a Republican deeply concerned or even afraid of what a Democratic Senate could mean for America, there's little to no utility in pairing that with a message of conspiracy about the integrity of elections. In a democracy, voting is the release mechanism for anger and discontent. When politicians take vot-ing off the table as a means to achieve change, removing hope from the equation for their constituents, what's left is not pretty. It's what we saw unleashed on the Capitol in January 2021. It's what we see in the most violent incidents involving the masked leftists of Antifa. No belief in the system. No hope for change by democratic means. What you get is indiscriminate violence.

During the Galactic Civil War, rebel leaders had a choice of their own in how they rallied the disaffected peoples of the galaxy to their cause. Senator Mon Mothma, Princess Leia, and Leia's adoptive father, Bail Organa of Alderaan, rose as the principal leaders of what is known as the Alliance to Restore the Republic, also known as the Rebel Alliance. This alliance was the culmination of roughly fifteen years of toil, sacrifice, and organizing on the part of these leaders. In the years following the formation of the Empire, there was dissent in several pockets of the galaxy. The problem was that individual rebel cells in this vast galaxy had little to no knowledge of one another's activities. To the best of their knowledge, they were acting alone, risking everything to stand up to a behemoth empire with little real hope of toppling it. The rebels would be "stronger together" if they knew of one another, so that was the first hurdle Mon Mothma, Leia, and Bail Organa had to clear...letting freedom-loving people of the galaxy know they were not alone.

After that, you have to keep the band together amid a fight against a brutal totalitarian enemy who doesn't recognize constructs such as "the rules of engagement" or civil rights. The Empire has no rule book. As a result, many dissidents asked if the Rebellion should be playing by the "rules" themselves. One such dissident was named Saw Gerrera, and he led a militant cell of rebels called the Partisans.

A REBEL WITHOUT A CAUSE

Seen on-screen in *Rogue One: A Star Wars Story* (2016), Saw Gerrera (Forest Whitaker) was a frightful figure in the imagination of both Imperial loyalists and the average citizen of the galaxy. He was clad in metallic armor and bore scars not only of resistance to the Empire, but also of the horrors of the Clone Wars. By the time we see him in *Rogue One*, Saw sports both a mechanical leg and a breathing apparatus that implies a collapsed lung or similar injury. Whenever he goes for his breathing tube, it's eerily reminiscent of Darth Vader's strained drawl of breath through his own oxygen delivery system, his iconic mask and black suit. Saw Gerrera, like Vader, has given up pieces of his humanity in the ongoing fight for freedom.

Gerrera serves as a foil to Mon Mothma and Leia's movement, a rebellion he often describes in air quotes when he's featured in animated series such as *Star Wars Rebels*. To him, Mothma is a guardian of the status quo, of politics and centrism. To Gerrera, Mothma is spineless and unwilling to do what must be done to take down the Empire. It's a common archetype in world history and in pop culture. Think Malcom X to Martin Luther King Jr., or Samuel Adams to his second cousin, John Adams, or Magneto to Professor Xavier in the X-Men series. Revolutionaries all of them, united by a similar goal or motivating sense of injustice, but divided on the means by which to achieve their end.

In *Rogue One*, we're treated to a little exposition about this rift with Gerrera from an exasperated Mon Mothma, who is struggling to keep the Rebel Alliance together amid increased pressure and violence from the Empire. "His militancy has caused the Alliance a great many problems," she says to the movie's chief protagonist and reluctant rebel agent, Jyn Erso.

Gerrera's Partisans are violent extremists known to kill civilians, torture their captives, and employ all sorts of other brutal tactics in their stand against the Empire. You won't find Saw waxing poetic about what he hopes to build after he defeats the Empire, because he has no vision for what comes next. What he understands, and somewhat to his credit, is that the Republic he once fought for during the Clone Wars became the Empire. He sees that through line as evidence the entire enterprise is rotten to the core. The Republic, the Empire—to him it is all the same. He's not wrong about this. But if your goal is to compel a galaxy to stand up to the objective evil of the Empire and throw off its oppression, would you take his little history lesson as inspiring…as a beacon of hope?

Doubtful. Hope isn't part of the equation for Saw. Just fear, righteous anger, and a burning hatred for the Empire. These things aren't enough to fuel a popular movement and founding of a new government, not in a galaxy far, far away and, in most cases, not in our own world either.

Saw Gerrera lives for the fight, but he doesn't have a cause that brings people together beyond their anger and fear. Successful movements require more.

WHAT WENT WRONG WITH THE "SUMMER OF LOVE"

Halfway through 2020, it seemed all but certain that the year would be defined by two things: the global pandemic and the

US presidential election. Then came May 25 and the killing of George Floyd by Minneapolis police. Floyd was detained by police for allegedly passing a counterfeit twenty dollar bill at Cup Foods, a neighborhood market on the south side of the city. One of the arresting officers, Derek Chauvin, had Floyd pinned to the ground beneath his knee, kneeling on him for nearly nine minutes. George Floyd died there on the pavement.

Minneapolis erupted. Soon the entire nation was swept up in protests, rioting, looting, and a mix of civil disobedience and outright violence. In the first week of June, at the peak of this turbulence, about half a million people had hit the streets in at least 550 spots across the United States.* In the midst of a pandemic, downtowns and government districts from coast to coast were burning.

This was a movement without a singular leader. Whereas the civil rights movement of the 1960s is popularly understood to have been led by Martin Luther King Jr., the #BlackLivesMatter movement encompassed a wide variety of civic and grassroots organizations, all pushing an agenda of racial justice. Some items in that agenda were moderate and aimed to work within the system to make meaningful changes in law to protect the civil rights of all Americans: banning no-knock warrants, breaking up police department unions, ending qualified immunity,

---

* Larry Buchanan, Quoctrung Bui, and Jugal K. Pate, "Black Lives Matter May Be the Largest Movement in U.S. History," *New York Times*, July 3, 2020, https://www.nytimes.com/interactive/2020/07/03/us/george-floyd-protests-crowd-size.html.

requiring a kind of liability insurance for police officers, and mandating that police use body cameras, among other things.

Then there was #AbolishThePolice and the burning of buildings, courtesy of radical groups like the anarchists of Antifa. These so-called "antifascists" reemerged in a big way in 2020, after generating headlines for a number of years, primarily for their antics on college campuses, such as shutting down events for conservative speakers or physical altercations with college Republicans. The militant left-wing group, its members clad in black and their faces concealed, has also been known to attack journalists and bystanders for documenting their activities or attempting to intervene.

Antifa is a popular boogeyman of conservative media, and not without cause. They're a scary group. The very fact that these violent, mostly white, and male militants mask their identities to the public is a big part of it. And it's a real gift to the defenders of the status quo. When Mon Mothma alluded to problems Saw Gerrera had been causing for the Alliance, some of that was related to military concerns, but most of it was PR. The Empire relished the opportunity to capture images of Gerrera's attacks and turn them into propaganda that smeared the entire rebel movement as one of terrorism and thuggery. Fear is an effective ally of the powerful, and political movements throughout history have had to reckon with this reality when challenging the government, law enforcement, or whatever powers that be.

When the Black Lives Matter movement and demonstrations peaked in June, support for their cause was measured by Pew

Research Center and sat at 67 percent for adults, a clear majority. By September that support had dropped by 29 percent, settling at 38 percent of adults.* That's a devastating drop-off in support. What began in 2013 as a movement in response to the killing of seventeen-year-old Trayvon Martin, a Black boy, and the subsequent acquittal of his killer, George Zimmerman, had come a long way and expanded its base of support from the suburbs to the boardrooms of the NFL and NBA. As the summer wound down, the civil unrest in Portland and Seattle was just getting started—what Seattle mayor Jenny Durkan described as a "summer of love" in regard to anarchists colonizing a part of downtown and dubbing it the "Capitol Hill Autonomous Zone," or CHAZ. It would have been totally comical if not for the violence that ran amok on those few blocks of downtown, culminating in a per capita crime rate that was fifty times that of Chicago.

These hotbeds of Antifa-organizing were teeming with random violence and street battles with police, supposedly in the name of racial justice. George Floyd's death was at this point something of an afterthought for what was happening on the streets. Rioters wielding makeshift clubs and shields were not pushing police reform, nor were they promoting policies that could be tied to the injustice that was perpetrated against George Floyd. Onlookers understood this wasn't about reform.

---

* Deja Thomas, "Support for Black Lives Matter has decreased since June but remains strong among Black Americans," Pew Research Center, September 16, 2020, https://www.pewresearch.org/fact-tank/2020/09/16/support-for-black-lives-matter-has-decreased-since-june-but-remains-strong-among-black-americans/.

Militant groups like Antifa believe that the United States itself was founded on white supremacy and that its constitution serves those same ends.

Antifa's goal is to burn it all down, and they make no effort to hide those intentions.

Unless you've read the *Communist Manifesto* and have some vague sense of what radical socialists like Antifa aim to build, you might be left asking yourself, "Where is hope in their movement"? Well, it's not there. The entire enterprise of dressing up in all black, brandishing weapons, and attacking agents of the state (police, federal officers) and civilians indiscriminately is an exercise in nihilism. There's nothing hopeful or aspirational about it, and as a result, its appeal is quite limited. This is why you'll never see an Antifa revolution take off.

BALANCING HOPE AND ANGER

There's a vocal contingent within the Star Wars fan community that pushes the idea that the franchise is exclusively a story about standing up to fascistic regimes. Those people aren't entirely wrong. Star Wars is definitely about the virtue of recognizing and facing down evil, and fascism is evil. But this debate tends to obscure at least two things. The first is the specific political orientation of the Empire and whether or not its specific brand of authoritarianism is purely fascism and not a hybrid that includes elements of communism and corporatism (among other things).

The second is what we've been exploring in this chapter about what it takes to win against oppressive regimes of any variety.

In any historical scenario you'll always be able to find real-life characters who fit the mold of either radical or realist, revolutionary or incrementalist. Star Wars and its clever inclusion of Saw Gerrera in the story of the Rebellion is no exception. And the timing was just right. In our own world, *Rogue One* had come just after the Bernie Sanders insurgency against Hillary Clinton in the 2016 Democratic presidential primaries. Now, we aren't talking about some sort of armed insurgency, of course, but a legitimately radical (and I don't mean that as a slur) alternative to the establishment figure and centrist that is Clinton. The timing didn't feel like a coincidence. The rise of Bernie Sanders and a more militant-Left politics came right on the heels of Barack Obama's tenure, a presidency many thought would be more progressive than it turned out to be. Obama spoke the language of the establishment, with an idealism about what America is and could be. He had his moments to the contrary. But at the end of the day, he was a guy whose 2006 book was entitled *The Audacity of Hope: Thoughts on Reclaiming the American Dream*. It wasn't titled *Irredeemable: Why the American Dream Never Really Existed*.

For all his flaws, Obama might have fit in at the table with Mon Mothma, Bail Organa, and the Rebel Alliance, fighting for a belief in what the Republic once stood for and could be again. On the other hand, it's hard to see the historical revisionists behind journalistic ambitions like the *New York Times'*

1619 Project, writer Nikole Hannah-Jones, for example, standing with anyone other than Saw Gerrera. To these kinds of thinkers, righteous anger is the primary currency of their politics. Anger can be enough to get people animated about change, but it tends to be a powder keg of emotion more prone to flaring up and burning out.

SAVING WHAT WE LOVE

Star Wars introduced a fracture into the formation of the Rebel Alliance for a reason. It was to reflect on how we choose to fight against forces of darkness, not just why. In *Episode VIII: The Last Jedi* (2017), Resistance fighter Rose Tico says to ex-storm-trooper-turned-freedom-fighter Finn, "That's how we're gonna win. Not by fighting what we hate. Saving what we love." Nicely put. But is Tico saying it's wrong to fight? Of course not.

When she says this, Rose Tico is lying amid a pile of rubble on the battlefield, after nearly losing her life to save Finn from the First Order's gigantic mechanical walkers. There's more than cheesy romanticism at play here: it's real wisdom.

There's fascinating research on the subject of what kind of rebellions or social movements are most successful, and why. Erica Chenoweth and Maria J. Stephan, in *Why Civil Resistance Works: The Strategic Logic of Nonviolent Conflict**, have compiled

---

* Erica Chenoweth and Maria J. Stephan, "Why Civil Resistance Works: The Strategic Logic of Nonviolent Conflict," Columbia University Press (website), December 2012, http://cup.columbia.edu/book/why-civil-resistance-works/9780231156820.

data on mass movements from 1900 to 2006, including 323 cases of maximalist campaigns and mobilizations to overthrow either an incumbent leader or pursue the establishment of an independent state.

In Star Wars terms, a "mobilization to overthrow either an incumbent leader" would be the Rebel Alliance against the Empire as seen in the original trilogy films. To "pursue the establishment of an independent state," would fit more into the mold of what the Separatist movement was trying to do in the prequel trilogy with their secession from the Republic and formation of the Confederacy of Independent Systems.

In Chenoweth and Stephan's research, unarmed and nonviolent techniques of pressure were far more likely to succeed, by a rate of nearly two to one. Success was defined in a somewhat narrow way. They required that a regime not only be overthrown but that a de facto legal state be set up shortly after without any foreign intervention. The importance of that last part, to Chenoweth and Stephan, was to point out that new regimes that met this criterion of success were more likely to end in democratic governance and not devolve into more civil war in the following years.

Nonviolence in *Why Civil Resistance Works* was characterized by coordinated boycotts, strikes, protests, go-slows, and economic and social noncooperation, and by engaging in these activities without causing physical harm or threat to bystanders. Now, let's be clear. The Rebel Alliance was not a "nonviolent" movement. It was an orchestrated military alliance that sought to build a coalition of the willing in hopes of cobbling together a large-enough fleet to do open battle with the Empire. In addition to conducting limited targeted engagements with the Empire, the rebels did this mostly through covert actions, such as stealing military hardware and broadcasting to the galaxy about the evils being perpetrated by Emperor Palpatine.

There's an old quote from Frederick Douglass that states, "The limits of tyrants are prescribed by the endurance of those whom they oppress." This is a timeless truth. Palpatine was ushered into power by thunderous applause and a popular mandate, a sort of tacit consent from the people of the galaxy that Palpatine should do what must be done to bring order and prosperity. Mon Mothma focused her energy on eroding the perception of galactic consent to the Empire's rule by making it known there was neither order nor prosperity, and on limiting the Rebellion's use of violence. The Empire's indiscriminate use of violence served as the means by which the Rebellion could delegitimize them. This kind of restraint on the part of the Rebellion is what expands the size and appeal of social movements. It also makes these movements more diverse.

Martin Luther King Jr. understood all of this and picked up much of it from veterans of Gandhi's movement in India against British colonialism. Living in the 2000s, it now seems somewhat like awarding participation trophies to laud white Americans for getting involved in the civil rights movement, which obviously was in the right, but the fact remains that nonviolent tactics and similar methods of showcasing the illegitimacy of enforcing racial segregation had the broadest appeal. That matters.

When faced with growing opposition, entrenched regimes—or whoever holds power—tend to employ a consistent tactic, whether it be in Star Wars, Gandhi's India, or the American South. Divide and conquer. Exploit divisions over tactics in the opposition movement, highlight their most violent actions, and consolidate support from onlookers who are apprehensive about change.

This is where hope comes in. Organizers, activists, politicians, and community leaders within democratic societies have to take on the challenge of expanding support for their causes. This can only be done credibly through consent, not force. Achieving this necessitates grappling with the facts on what motivates people to join up in the first place. Messages rooted in anger, despair, and nihilism don't have a strong track record.

Rebellions are built on hope.

BUILT ON HOPE

So I ask you again, do you have hope? If you don't, it's okay. You're not broken, and there's nothing wrong with you. It's important to be good to yourself and know that others like you have felt that same sense of despair. That's why Star Wars has always stood out to me as a beacon of light in a changing and tumultuous dark world. Luke Skywalker's loneliness on Tatooine, Princess Leia's choice to be bold even after the annihilation of Alderaan . . . there will always be people who feel this way and leaders who face what seem like insurmountable odds. In the Star Wars universe, what each generation of characters seems to face is the life cycle of democracy and self-governance in the face of dark forces pulling the galaxy back toward totalitarianism. We're at a turning point ourselves, aren't we? I don't think you have to be a liberal or a conservative, a Republican or a Democrat, to look at the state of the world and see that democracy, rule of law, and liberty are neither guaranteed nor a natural state of affairs. There are new challenges to them for every generation.

The Last Jedi's chief villain, Supreme Leader Snoke, said to aspiring Jedi and Resistance fighter Rey, "Darkness rises and light to meet it." Of course, Snoke hoped to snuff that light out, but he demonstrated an understanding there about how each of our galaxies works. Change is guaranteed. The choice we have is how to face change and challenge darkness.

"Returning hate for hate multiplies hate, adding deeper darkness to a night already devoid of stars. Darkness cannot drive out darkness; only light can do that," Martin Luther King Jr. wrote in his 1963 book, *Strength to Love*. He goes on, "Hate cannot drive out hate; only love can do that. Hate multiplies hate, violence multiplies violence, and toughness multiplies toughness in a descending spiral of destruction."*

I can't think of a more Star Wars-esque reminder from our own history. I can't think of a more compelling reason to hold on to hope as a virtue, even when it is not something we feel every day.

---

* Martin Luther King Jr., *Strength to Love* (New York: Harper & Row, 1963).

Tips: How to Find Hope When
It's Hard to See

- **Hope and optimism are contagious.** While some people have particularly strong antibodies to this way of seeing the world, it makes a huge difference who you spend time with and who is dominating your social media news feed. My mom always used to say, "You are what you eat," and when it comes to information and perspective, that checks out. Make time for optimists in your life.

- **Gratitude and hope are interconnected.** Late in life it can be hard to learn gratitude, short of a near-death experience in which you realize how temporary this thing called life can be. Let's avoid that. Instead, practice mindfulness. Whether it be meditation or prayer, there's something powerful about focusing on your breath moving in and out of your lungs and on counting your blessings.

- **Fear can majorly get in the way of cultivating hope in your life.** Fear of rejection, fear of failure or loss. You're going to have to move past it in certain places to see this thing called hope, that light at the end of whatever tunnel you're in.

- **Don't let bad news get you down.** If you see local news that worries you, maybe a carjacking, an assault, or an incident of a hate crime, look into whether it's part of a trend. News thrives on drama and tragedy, and news programs often won't tell you that something horrific was an anomaly if it conflicts with the bias of their institutions. Do your own homework. Look at trends.

CHAPTER 5

REDEMPTION OR A RECKONING

"The greatest teacher, failure is."

—Yoda

REDEMPTION

THE CONCLUSION OF *Episode VI: Return of the Jedi* (1983), the final installment of the original Star Wars trilogy, is one of my absolute favorite moments in all of the Star Wars saga. What's not to like? There's the dazzling space battle when against all the odds the rebels take out the Death Star for a second time. There's the climactic duel between Luke Skywalker and Darth Vader when Vader turns back to the light. And to top it all off, there's a raucous victory celebration on Endor complete with fuzzy, dancing killer bears. But there's a scene in the saga's final act that always gets me, and it's a much quieter moment.

It's a conversation that Luke has with Vader, alone on a landing platform on the forest moon of Endor. Having earlier been in the dark about Vader's true identity, Luke now knows the dark lord was once Anakin Skywalker. Luke has accepted that this metallic ghoul is in fact his long-lost father. Young Skywalker attempts to rattle Vader and shake him from the path he's chosen. He tells Vader that there is still another way.

"You can't do this. I feel the conflict within you. Let go of your hate!" Luke says to Vader. There's a somber pause. "It's too late for me, son," Vader says back. From there, Vader beckons stormtroopers to take Luke away to be presented to the evil emperor. It's a death sentence for the young Jedi if he doesn't join forces with the Empire.

After Luke is gone, Vader walks slowly to the glass window of the walkway, breathing heavily as he always does. He leans forward and grabs the handrail and stares blankly out at the forest before him. Not even Vader's mask can hide the thoughts tumbling through his mind.

Luke was right. There is conflict within him.

Star Wars fans today are familiar with Anakin's story from the prequels. But this scene in its original context is supposed to be the first real glimpse audiences see of the man behind the dark mask, the fallen Jedi trapped beneath the black cape and life-support system of Darth Vader.

Vader just stares. You're left wondering what it is he's thinking. What calculation is he making? Is his conscience stirred by what's about to happen to Luke? To say "It's too late for me" is a fatalistic response to Luke's invitation to walk away from the dark side. He could have said something like "I'm happy with where I am, thank you very much" or "I've never felt better." But he didn't because that's not true. Vader is miserable; he just doesn't see another way.

In his despair, Vader opts to continue what he's been doing since the day he first donned the black armor and breathing apparatus. He doubles down and chooses to reside in his shame. Redemption, he feels, is unattainable.

Even the best of us can relate. When you look around the world, do you see a culture of personal growth, forgiveness, and redemption on the rise? Or do you see one of vengeance, vindictiveness, and retribution taking hold of our discourse and behavior? Perhaps "cancel culture" comes to mind, or criminal justice policies that prioritize harsh punishment over rehabilitation. When I talk to friends, whether they be left, right, or center, I hear the same worry—that we're on the latter path. We agree that it didn't always used to be this way, and that something has changed.

It's no coincidence that politics has polarized and become so extreme at the same time our societies are adopting social media as the primary mode of interaction. Religious affiliation and belief wane as the Twitterverse waxes. The resulting shift in the ideological tide has swept us off our feet. And now we're all at sea. How do we think about our place in the world? How should we treat one another? Believe it or not, about such things Star Wars holds a lot of wisdom for us.

This chapter is about redemption—the idea that when we've messed up, it's not the end of our story. Often confused with "forgiveness" or "atonement," redemption is tied to our capacity for hope. It's something we believe in, more than it is something we do. To give up on redemption is to resign ourselves to living life in the wreckage of our forefathers or the life that we've created for ourselves, like Darth Vader.

Star Wars is a story that believes in redemption. It is not just a space opera about the road to hell good intentions can lead you down; it's also a story about the road back home. Maybe that road leads back to family, or to friends, or just to a mirror in which a person who has done terrible things can learn to look at themselves again and not despise what they see. Darth Vader finds redemption in the faith and goodwill of an estranged son. Ben Solo, Vader's grandson, finds redemption in the mercy of a rival, and the unconditional love of his parents. To a culture mired in such vitriolic division, where no matter what you do or say it seems there's always judgment waiting for you, these stories of redemption are absolutely vital. In our own lives we must fight to preserve what little appetite our culture has left for redemption and do the hard work of building it back up again.

A society that underrates the value of redemption is not a society any of us should want to live in. Because while we may want to hold people who do us wrong accountable or "cancel" them, we'll ultimately be defined by how we treat those who have fallen and are looking for a hand up. Redemption has long been a key element of America's story. It's the pursuit of progress—not perfection—and a recognition of our errors that offer us a path to peace with one another and within ourselves. This has been true in America since the founding, and moving forward, this is how we fix our country and the world.

Star Wars isn't going to solve everything. The saga from a

long time ago in a galaxy far, far away couldn't possibly lead us to a new order or to global peace and harmony. But it does point us to some key concepts that, if we take them to heart, could help us on our journey through our flawed world.

So let's jump in! To start, let's consider a scandal central to the Star Wars universe: the bad guys get away with murder and genocide.

SPACE NAZIS AND SITH DEPLORABLES

Do Darth Vader and Kylo Ren amount to "space Nazis"? Star Wars fans love to debate these kinds of things. They're both militaristic leaders of expansionary, brutal regimes and have a long track record of war crimes and participation in acts of genocide. Very bad stuff! Nevertheless, both Darth Vader and Kylo Ren experience redemption arcs in their stories. They come back to the light and lay down their ruby-red lightsabers in an effort to finally do the right thing. And both die in some semblance of peace.

Darth Vader intervenes in the torture of his son, Luke Skywalker, at the hands of Emperor Palpatine and his Force lightning. In a move guaranteed to short-circuit his mechanical breathing apparatus, Vader picks his evil master up and throws him down a pit within the Death Star. He relinquishes the dark side and has Luke remove his mask. Vader embraces his true identity, and mere moments before his death, the audience witnesses the return of the long-lost Jedi, Anakin Skywalker. Later, at the celebration on Endor, he shows up as a Force ghost, a feat accomplished by only the best of Jedi who've become one with the Force.

Years later, Vader's grandson, Ben Solo, lives out the same story. Just as his grandfather did, Solo turns to the dark side and develops an alter ego. Whereas Vader was born out of tragic loss and anger, Kylo Ren was born out of confusion and betrayal. Yet just as Vader eventually finds his way back to the light, so, too, does Ren. In the end, he even fights the same villain. In the climactic scene of *Episode IX: The Rise of Skywalker* (2019), Ren helps Rey conquer Palpatine once and for all, giving his life in the process. At his death, Ren vanishes—an indication that he, too, has become one with the Force.

What gives? How is this fair? Both Vader and Ren are guilty. They've done horrible things and are both responsible for atrocities, including but not limited to overseeing the slaughter of millions throughout the galaxy and murdering their own kin. They're monsters.

Still, despite their monstrosity, most fans (myself among them) yearn for them to change. Why is that?

I don't know a single Star Wars fan who hungers for Darth Vader to have "gotten what he deserved" or to have been executed for his crimes. But that could be because *Return of the Jedi* came out nearly forty years ago.

The discourse around Kylo Ren, however, is noticeably different. Perhaps it's merely the existence of Twitter making divisive fan debates more visible than ever before, but I'd argue something has changed within the hearts of the audience.

REDEMPTION OR A RECKONING

As we approached 2019 and the release of the sequel trilogy's final installment, *Episode IX: The Rise of Skywalker*, a dialogue began online about what kind of message it sent to fans if Kylo Ren found redemption in the end. You had one segment of fandom arguing that Kylo Ren was the embodiment of privilege, a white male of royal blood with loving parents who *still* chose to join a quasi-fascist regime and oppress the galaxy. This slice of woke fans filtered Star Wars through their politics of social justice and looked at what Star Wars chose to do with Kylo as a signal of whether Disney was a committed ally in the fight against "white supremacy." Take that narrative as you will. Whether he's an embodiment of white supremacy or just a symbol of someone's fall from grace, what's indisputable is that Kylo is the worst of the worst.

Still, the debate yielded a more viral sensation: #Bendemption. An opposing corner of fandom stepped forward as super fans of Ben Solo, the boy beneath the mask of Kylo Ren, and formed an online community around the hope that Ben could come back to the light. These fans also really wanted Ben to be redeemed so he could hook up with Rey, but that's beside the point.

If you thought *Episode VIII: The Last Jedi* (2017) was divisive, watch your step wading into the #Bendemption discourse online. It's a microcosm of a few different debates, but most important, it's a raging battle over the merits and pitfalls of cancel culture.

You can count me as a member of Team Bendemption. We

want hope in our Star Wars, and in the end, we more or less got it. And that's one of the great things about the Star Wars universe: the accessibility of redemption for its worst characters is ultimately a commentary on what's possible for you, the audience. You may not be an intergalactic fascist, but if the Kylo Rens of the fictional world aren't redeemable, then maybe you aren't either.

Carving out space in our popular culture for this message is becoming increasingly important, as matters in the real world have become quite perilous.

Remember the Bible story in which Jesus stops a mob from stoning to death a woman accused of adultery? It's in the Gospel of John, when Christ intervenes and says, "He that is without sin among you, let him first cast a stone" (John 8:7). The crowd had intended to kill the woman in accordance with Mosaic law, the ultimate cancelation. But Jesus' challenge to the mob—to look in the mirror and judge themselves first—stops them in their tracks. Their judgment of the accused woman was correct, but still, no one was willing to be the first person to claim the mantle of purity and serve as executioner.

If Jesus were around today, he'd be very busy.

In our world, we are all of us just one tweet away from a virtual stoning at the hands of a mob looking for any wrongdoing in our past that can be dredged up online. Mean tweets from when you were fifteen? Photos of you dressed up as a Native American for a school play in fourth grade? The Twitter mob knows no statute of limitations.

The hard truth is that we're all just one slip up from being branded: "sinner," "adulterer," "racist," "sexist," "screwup"— "space Nazi." For this reason, we need to believe in redemption— the kind you see in the character arcs of Star Wars villains. Yes, the Star Wars movies are just stories, but they're stories we need to hear. They're stories that extend grace to the outcast and hope for anyone who's not just slipped up—but done real harm. And unless you really think you're blameless enough to pick up that first stone and merk an adulteress, I think you'd agree that stories of absolution have a way of always hitting home.

SAVE YOUR APOLOGIES

"Cancel culture" is largely considered to have started on elite college campuses in the mid-2010s. A small but energized band of typically Far-Left activists would push to ostracize someone from social or professional life, for transgressions real or imagined, or blockade well-known conservative figures from appearing on campus for events small or large. Back in 2014, former secretary of state Condoleezza Rice was supposed to give a commencement address at the Rutgers University graduation ceremony. Student activists protested. They staged a sit-in outside the office of the university president, chanting, "Cancel Condi." Rice was no stranger to student protest, having experienced it throughout her tenure in the George W. Bush administration for her role in the Iraq War.

This is fair game in a free country. Most people understood

this to be the case. People can dislike you, there can be disagreement and dissent, and both parties ultimately have to deal with one another's existence. Condoleezza Rice eventually bowed out of the Rutgers commencement, offering in a statement, "I have defended America's belief in free speech and the exchange of ideas. These values are essential to the health of our democracy."*

Things have changed a lot since that time. I remember hearing these stories back then and thinking, "These are isolated incidents," "College activists grow up eventually," "Once these kids graduate and enter the workforce, they'll adjust to reality."

I could not have been more wrong.

Left to metastasize within institutions of higher education, universities have exported the ethos of cancel culture to the highest rungs of journalism, media, and corporate America. The idea of "discomfort" with ideas evolved steadily to speech equaling violence. Team Bendemption may have won in the Star Wars universe, but in the real world the mob usually gets its way. And when it does, it's never pretty. You've probably heard a few cancelation stories yourself. As I write this, the news cycle has latched on to the latest cancel culture story involving Alexi McCammond, a young Black journalist who after departing the website Axios was hired to be the editor in chief of *Teen Vogue*.

Her tenure there was short-lived. The staff of *Teen Vogue* "resurfaced" tweets of McCammond's from when she was

---

* Emma G. Fitzsimmons, "Condoleezza Rice Backs Out of Rutgers Speech After Student Protests," *New York Times*, May 4, 2014, https://www.nytimes.com/2014/05/04/nyregion/rice-backs-out-of-rutgers-speech-after-student-protests.html.

seventeen years old. The posts were objectively racist, directed at Asians. But here's the thing: these tweets had already been brought up in the public square two years earlier. She'd already been exposed, already apologized publicly, and already suffered for her past sin. Yet, in an effort to quell the uprising at *Teen Vogue*, McCammond apologized again in the strongest possible terms.

The Asian American Journalists Association came to McCammond's defense, somewhat.* They condemned her past remarks, but made pretty clear in their press release that this was in the past and that instead of dropping the ax on McCammond, *Teen Vogue* should look to elevate Asian Americans in their workplace and audience:

> We denounce the racist tweets. But we also believe that there is room for everyone to acknowledge, learn and grow from past mistakes. We support the long overdue appointment of more journalists of color and women for top leadership positions. And we believe in this moment's potential for difficult conversations around allyship, and learning how we can better support each other—we spoke with McCammond and the chief diversity officer at Conde Nast about their efforts to understand and address our community's concerns. We look forward to continuing our

---

* Asian American Journalists Association, "AAJA calls on Condé Nast to ensure its commitment to Asian American and Pacific Islander communities and employees," March 10, 2021, https://www.aaja.org/2021/03/10/aaja-calls-on-conde-nast-to-ensure-its-commitment-to-asian-american-and-pacific-islander-communities-and-employees/.

dialogue and being a resource and thought partner as they work to build an even more inclusive newsroom and produce thoughtful and equitable coverage.

But none of this mattered. The staff at *Teen Vogue* weren't looking for a mea culpa: they wanted to see McCammond's head roll. She backed out of the job before she'd even set up her office.

McCammond's story is bad news for anyone who's ever fallen from grace. Not only will your faults be exposed and not only will you be ostracized for them, but there will be nothing you can do to make it right. If you tell that to someone for long enough, eventually they'll start to believe it. They'll begin to think, like Darth Vader, "It is too late for me." And that's when folks embrace the dark side.

That decision to embrace the darkness and infamy is something that worries me a lot, actually. As religious belief has declined and social trends like cancel culture continue to rise, the eagerness of some to toss out the virtue of asking for forgiveness is troubling.

There's a lot of powerful people out there now saying, "NEVER APOLOGIZE," because the cancelers aren't looking to forgive, only control. Instead, the reasoning goes, we should be vigilant and strive to keep what Obi-Wan Kenobi might have called the high ground. That's a smart tactic if you're looking to win a fight, but it has a corrosive effect on the culture. It walls us off from the possibility of redemption.

We tend to favor the path of least resistance. Have you noticed people around you becoming more callous and attached to their politics or their worst opinions? I sure have. I tend to believe this happens because finding kinship with "the other side" or admitting you were wrong tends to be way harder and more thankless than just sticking to your guns, embracing the darkness, and being the villain your opponents believe you to be.

As Vader's and Ren's stories show, the feeling that "it's too late" to make amends can be extremely destructive. To fight that feeling in our culture, we should follow Luke Skywalker's example, sensing the good in others regardless of what evil they've committed and extending grace to the fallen.

REDEMPTION ISN'T FAIR

Here again we're confronted with the unfairness of it all. Though it's been around for thousands of years, wherever you see it redemption is still something of a scandal. Let's go way back in time for a moment.

In ancient Egypt, there was this practice known as the Duat, where the deceased had their heart weighed on a scale against a feather known as the feather of Ma'at. The feather, likely plucked from ostriches, represented truth and justice and was believed to possess a supernatural quality to assess the righteousness of the heart on the scale. Your purity, respect for the law, and overall goodness were determinable in this ritual. What happened to you in the afterlife boiled down to the weight of your heart versus the feather.

Take a wild guess how that played out for most of the deceased.

Fast-forward a few thousand years to about 27 AD, and Jesus Christ is on the scene offering something different from the rituals and law of the ancient world. The human heart is understood at birth to be overweight, your debt impossibly large, your bar tab of blunders wildly run up. Redemption in Christ through the blood shed at his crucifixion equated to an interest-free payment on the debt. You can't pay him back. All that's expected is recognition, gratitude, and acceptance.

Accepting Christ's sacrifice breeds peace in your heart, making it light as a feather.

As seen in the Christian faith, this peace and redemption is an unearned gift that requires an act of atonement by God himself. Christ is born unto a virgin and lives a perfect life only to die by brutal crucifixion as a blood sacrifice for the sins of the world. Jesus, the very son of God, dies so that we can live. Such a substitution is the epitome of injustice.

There is no mathematical logic to a belief system that says, for example: "Darth Vader...I know he murdered dozens of Jedi younglings, subjugated entire worlds, and shrouded the galaxy in darkness, but if he just accepts Christ as his Savior, then of course he should get to enjoy eternal life and the glorious bounty of Heaven."

That makes no sense. Yet it's this incalculable gift—the grace coming from an outside source—that holds the power to change lives.

ATONEMENT ON STARKILLER BASE

In the original Star Wars trilogy, we see this kind of goodwill change Darth Vader's heart as Luke extends grace to his father. In the sequels, we see the relationship reversed as Han's unconditional love for his son eventually leads Kylo Ren to relinquish the dark side and live as Ben Solo again.

Han Solo knows his son, Ben Solo, is suffering under the heavy metallic mask of Kylo Ren when he confronts him on a catwalk within Starkiller Base in *Episode VII: The Force Awakens* (2015). The Star Wars audience knows instinctively that the saga's mentors and father figures are often marked for death, but as I sat in the theater on the opening night of *The Force Awakens*, even I wasn't ready for what would happen.

"Take that mask off. You don't need it," Han says to his son.

"What do you think you'll see if I do?"

"The face of my son," says Han, without hesitation. You might think you know who you are. But no one knows you like Dad.

Hear the echoes of Vader in Ren's reply: "It's too late," he says.

"No, it's not. Leave here with me. Come home," Han answers. "We miss you."

The lighting in this scene is particularly effective. Ren's face is lit in blue light from above, red from below—a symbol of his conflicting identities. As Kylo Ren struggles to delve deeper into the darkness, Ben Solo is called to the light. For the villain, this conflict is unbearable. To end the struggle, Ren must sever all ties with Solo. But that's not something he can do as long as his parents are alive. Ben Solo lives as long as Han and Leia continue to call him home.

"I'm being torn apart," says Ben. "I know what I have to do, but I don't know if I have the strength to do it. Will you help me?"

"Anything," Han answers.

Ben unclips his lightsaber from his belt and hands it to Han. Both men hold the handle of the blade in silence. Then the blue light fades, Kylo's face is bathed in red, and the budding dark lord does the unthinkable. He murders his father.

When you watch this scene, you can read it a dozen different ways, and I'll admit I see different things each time I view *The Force Awakens*. But it's not a stretch to think Ben asks Han to help him fulfill the deed of patricide and that Han intentionally allows his son to take his life, without resistance. Han is a Christ figure, dying for the sins of his son.

It's the ultimate act of unconditional love, to let Ben's journey run its course. And it turns out to be an effective antidote to the darkness in young Solo. Once Ben experiences the pain of that deed and sees just how unconditional a parent's love can be, his days wearing the mask of Kylo Ren are numbered.

He's broken by it, and while Ben Solo does delve deeper into the darkness, still, his mother lives. It's her love for him and the grace extended by his enemy, Rey, that helps hammer his redemption arc home. That kind of love and mercy is hard to come by in the real world, and an increasing number of people are unlikely to even understand where these kinds of moral stories come from.

A KINGDOM ON EARTH

By and large, the Western world was built with the Christian story as its foundation for understanding human nature. This is as much as to say its civilizations embraced humanity as being broken and in need of fixing. Foundations matter. Star Wars, while most heavily inspired by Eastern religions such as Hinduism and Buddhism, draws in part from this tradition as well. George Lucas said of the saga's spirituality, "I see 'Star Wars' as taking all the issues that religion represents and trying to distill them down into a more modern and accessible construct."*

"Construct" is a good word for capturing the ways in which we're primed to see the world. If you've grown up in the West, America in particular, you're part of society that holds itself accountable to a God in an afterlife. With the exception of staunch atheists, we skew toward a belief in divine judgment rather than toward our fellow man being the ultimate moral authority in the universe.

Christians are still the most populous religious group in the world, dominating five continents as the most-adhered-to religion. The runners-up, however, are the unaffiliated. The

---

* George Lucas, "Of Myth And Men," interview by Bill Moyers, *Time*, April 18, 1999, transcript, http://content.time.com/time/magazine/article/0,9171,23298-2,00.html.

nonreligious. The secular. And this is changing the balance: 2021 was the first year, in eight decades of surveying American's religiosity, that Gallup found fewer than 50 percent of respondents were members of a church, mosque, or synagogue. Maybe you think that's good; maybe you don't. But regardless of your opinion, there's a side effect of religion's decline that we all have to reckon with.

The rise of the nonreligious as a majority group shifts the burden of accountability, atonement, and justice away from the divine and toward the immediate dominion of man. "Well, that's nothing new," you might say. "We've had a justice system here in the United States for centuries."

True, but an American is not asked to put their hand on the Bible and say, "I swear to tell the truth, the whole truth, and nothing but the truth, so help me God" for no reason. That happens because our nation has an institutionalized but fading belief that no matter what happens in a courtroom, we ultimately answer to the Big Man upstairs. Without that, the stakes of what we do on Earth are raised tremendously. And that's not good.

To be human is to do harm to others. As a species, we're beautifully designed wrecking balls with passionate hearts and wild minds. We mess things up daily despite our best intentions. In light of this, whether you're a firm atheist or a Muslim, Christian, or Jew, the establishment of organized belief systems that hinge on redemption being achievable seems like one of the more rational things mankind has ever done.

TRADING REDEMPTION FOR RECKONING

When you take all of this into account, is it really surprising that the American psyche has taken such an ugly turn? Politics is becoming toxic, and redemption stories are becoming countercultural. Where are we? And how do we get out of the pit that we're digging ourselves into?

The conservative Right has some serious problems, chief among them the crisis of faith we've just reviewed. It's resulted in thousands of supposedly Christian Americans being drawn into the QAnon conspiracy theory, like an X-Wing caught in the Death Star's tractor beam. Absent hope and carrying a hollow belief in the Kingdom of Heaven, the Right has run away with a cult dedicated to trying to save the world from satanic cannibals—even though Christian belief would tell you the world can't be saved. But I want to focus on the political Left for now, to better understand the battles we're seeing all over TV news and on our city streets.

Let's be honest in saying that the political Left has long had a standoffish relationship with the idea of American exceptionalism. They're more skeptical of patriotic displays, flag-waving— all that kind of stuff. This makes sense if you look at the 1960s and '70s, the Vietnam War, and the civil rights movement as one of major sorting periods in American political history. The Democratic Party absorbed a majority of the Black vote after the franchise was extended, and the anti-war movement created a generation of Democrats molded in opposition to a considerably corrupt, law-and-order Republican president, Richard Nixon.

Star Wars' creator, George Lucas, is among that cohort of Democrats whose appreciation for the country went hand in hand with distrust. But while that generation undoubtedly saw the worst of America—the pointless war abroad, segregation, the fire hoses in Birmingham, an active Ku Klux Klan terrorizing Blacks in the South, numerous political assassinations, and national panic over Soviet Communism—they also saw things rapidly improve.

America has changed radically, both in speed and in substance. Interracial relationships went from being taboo (or illegal in some places) to commonplace in just a few decades, right alongside huge decreases in the prevalence of racially prejudiced viewpoints and a surge in support for things such as gay marriage.

But when you grow up in that period of progress, it's easy to take for granted those advancements. And that's exactly what is happening right now.

The murder of George Floyd in the spring of 2020 by a Minneapolis police officer lit the country on fire, both morally and literally. Protests led by a much younger generation of leftists came with a rapid tossing out of America's redemptive narrative, the same narrative that put Barack Obama in the White House and kept him there for eight years. What has replaced it is a new "r" word: reckoning.

Almost overnight, America went from pursuing a newfound ideal of colorblindness and racial harmony to a hyperfocus on racial difference. What started with the rise of Black Lives Matter, something I'd argue is a defensible campaign, quickly morphed into things such as the *New York Times*' 1619 Project and the rapid proliferation of Critical Race Theory among academics and schools. The latter looks at racism less as a surmountable state of mind and more as a preexisting medical condition tied to being white. And if you harbor views that go against Left politics, well, they're not mere differences of opinion. Those views are evidence of internalized whiteness, an incurable ailment treatable only by buying the right books and keeping up with the ever-changing vocabulary of social justice academia.

The Left's relationship to America's founding sin, slavery and racial subjugation, went from being a delicately formed scab to being an open wound courting infection. And it happened very fast. The election of Donald Trump in 2016 obviously played a part in this.

I want to concede that, on the one hand, it's vital that America be vocal and proud of its transformation since its founding, but on the other hand, there has not been enough done to fully recognize the darkness buried just inches beneath all the progress.

Any Star Wars fan can tell you: wrestling that darkness is essential if you want to move forward.

ENTERING THE CAVE

In *Episode V: The Empire Strikes Back* (1980), Luke is training to be a Jedi with Yoda on the swamp world of Dagobah. One day,

Luke feels an energy coming from a nearby cave, which Yoda says is a place shrouded in the dark side of the Force.

Luke asks what is inside the cave, to which Yoda replies, "Only what you take with you."

The cave is a popular metaphorical device in fiction going back as far as the Greek classics of the eighth century BC. In Book VII of the *Republic*, Plato describes human existence in terms of people being chained up in a cave since birth, made only to see shadows cast on the wall in front of them for their entire life. The story goes on to explain how when someone is then freed from that cave and exposed to the real world beyond those walls, it is both frightening and alienating. Storytelling ever since has been influenced by Plato's understanding of the cave. It's a place where reality is fungible and a person's emotional baggage can manifest itself as more than a mere shadow cast on the wall.

Heroes enter all sorts of caves and experience this blending of truth and fiction. Sometimes it's an experience of fantasy and ecstasy, and other times terror. It's a device that's commonly used to show what lies dormant within the protagonist. Their fears, desires, weaknesses, and wants are put on full display. In Luke's case, he runs right into Darth Vader, a specter who very recently killed Luke's mentor, Obi-Wan Kenobi. The ghost is evidence of Luke's burning desire for vengeance—justice, if you will.

Luke duels Vader and wins, decapitating the Sith lord almost effortlessly. The villain's helmet rolls to the ground and bursts open, revealing Vader's identity. Only it's no stranger Luke sees behind the mask.

It's his own face. And now Yoda's point is clear. Luke, in all his goodness and strength of heart, could become like Vader if he isn't careful. He is no knight in shining armor; he is just another person one push or stumble away from wickedness. When you understand that about yourself, when you recognize both what you're capable of and what you have already done, only then can you start to make peace with it. Only then can you *maybe* make things right.

ATONEMENT AND ACCOUNTABILITY

I'd argue that conservative America needs to spend some time in the cave with Luke on Dagobah. The pursuit of a colorblind America is a worthy one, but it creates a blind spot in recognizing what the Left calls "structural racism"—the simple idea that racism lingers not just in our attitudes or actions, but also in the way our institutions work. A commonly cited example of this type of racism is the 1986 Anti-Drug Abuse Act, which criminalized crack cocaine and powder cocaine differently. Crack was a known street drug running rampant in the Black community. Powdered cocaine was the drug of more affluent whites. The sentencing disparity between the two was nearly one hundred to one, an inequity that wasn't addressed until 2011 under the Fair Sentencing Act.

Today, there's a potent air of denialism about stuff like this on the political Right, and it doesn't serve them well.

As a nation of individuals, the United States is remarkably not racist. We live, play, work, and love among each other, across racial lines, in ways that are unprecedented in human history. We're a multiracial democratic republic, and compared to the rest of the world we're doing well. But our government, the institution that represents and embodies the collective, has largely shirked its moral responsibility to atone for its wrongs, whether that be slavery, Jim Crow, or the ill-conceived War on Drugs.

What did we really do as a country after the Civil Rights Act of 1964 was signed into law? As far as I can tell, America simply carried on with business as usual. And in the absence of any official reparations for slavery, disenfranchisement, and legal discrimination, individual Americans are increasingly the ones trying to make things right regarding a travesty in which they played no part. It's why Nike and Coca-Cola are now on the front lines of racial justice, forcing this reconciliation into every corner of our lives—places where we'd much rather be left alone.

No matter how aggravating the social justice messaging gets, it's never the right move to deny the faults of our nation. We've got to embrace these sins, seek redemption, and move forward.

So how do we do that? How do we conquer this kind of ever-present darkness and live out happier lives? When Zeno, the intellectual founder of the Stoic philosophy, arrived in Athens around 312 BC and began to pursue a new life as a thinker, he asked an oracle to tell him how to live well. It has been said the oracle told him, "To live the best life, you should have conversation with the dead." Star Wars knows all about this. So now we're going to take a look at the mechanics of Force-ghosting, the Star Wars universe's ultimate sign of closure, wisdom, and peace.

FORCE-GHOSTING

Accountability and atonement matter. It's why Catholics confess their sins to a priest; it's why Muslims practice *tawbah*, repentance between them and their maker; and it's why America's in a pickle today. Most Americans today are not religious, in the sense that they neither attend houses of worship nor practice a faith. That means they're lacking a fundamental understanding of the world that allows for redemption and atonement. That's one of the reasons we need Star Wars and stories like it so badly: to bridge the gap between the religious and the secular and to transpose the wisdom of the world's religions into a key that everyone can hear.

Star Wars doesn't just borrow from the Abrahamic religions. Take Force-ghosting, for example—that is, how a select few in the Star Wars lore have lived on after death and been able to physically manifest themselves to counsel and advise future generations of Jedi.

It's not just the holiest of Jedi who return as Force ghosts. Darth Vader appears as a Force ghost at the end of *Return of the Jedi*. This is troubling at first to many of us whose views on redemption have been shaped by Judeo-Christian philosophy.

Why should Vader get to live on after death while his thousands of victims are just gone? The same can be asked of Kylo Ren, who vanishes into the Force upon his death. How are these villains worthy of such honor?

Well, they aren't. The inner peace that Force-ghosting and Force-vanishing symbolizes isn't something you achieve by being good. You don't earn it in that way.

This is where George Lucas draws on Hindu and Buddhist tradition to inform the rules of the Star Wars universe. These Eastern religions teach that to achieve peace you have to battle and tame your own inner chaos.

This philosophy was manifested in a story line of the Star Wars animated series *The Clone Wars*. Long story short, sometime between Episodes II and III, Master Yoda hears the voice of Qui-Gon Jinn reaching out to him from beyond, and at its behest, our favorite tiny green Jedi takes off across the galaxy. He's led to a metaphysical realm inhabited by ethereal beings who present him with several trials to prove himself worthy of eternal life through the Force.

What Yoda learns is that the power to conquer death requires a head-on confrontation with his own inner darkness. During Yoda's trials the ethereal beings that possess the knowledge of the Force ghost power say to him, "You are the beast, and the beast is you."

Yoda must duel a dark version of himself. It's in that confrontation that he realizes that the mangled, frightening, red-eyed being he's fighting is no alien creature but his other half—just as much an authentic part of him as the gentle and kind mentor helping Jedi pupils every day in the temple on Coruscant.

Once Yoda chooses to see his dark self as an equal, the Guardians say to him, "You have conquered your hubris."

HUBRIS AND "THE SHADOW"

When you acknowledge and accept your darkness, your brokenness, and your capacity for wickedness—only then will you truly know yourself. The famed Swiss psychiatrist Carl Jung called this thing within us "the shadow," but he thought of it less like a Dr. Jekyll and Mr. Hyde situation and more like a simple affirmation of your blind spots. Jung said denying the existence of those blind spots is what gives them power, feeds them, and lets them grow in strength. In essence, he might argue that you have to engage the shadow and hold dominion over it in order to keep it in check.

That's what Yoda does when he lays down his pride and his Jedi-like sense of purity to conquer his hubris. By the end of his journey, he's discovered the secret that allows him to live on after death and advise the next generation of Jedi. We see him appear several decades after his passing, in *Episode VIII: The Last Jedi* (2017), when Luke is in desperate need of guidance to help Rey.

Fans of Star Wars tend to talk about Force ghosts as if they were in heaven, as if this life after death were a cosmic reward for good behavior, a thing reserved for the "good people" and not the bad. This just isn't so.

Anakin Skywalker's and Ben Solo's redemptions are deeply personal affairs. The Force does not deem these characters "pure" by any means. Ben Solo vanishes into the Force because he's conquered his shadow. Anakin lives on after death as a Force ghost because he has put to rest an alter ego that had seized the steering wheel of his life all those years ago. Both villains achieve peace through a reckoning with their inner darkness that results in balance and harmony.

America is in the middle of such a reckoning today. Indeed, our nation's failures have never before been so widely acknowledged. And we should see that as a good thing. Our dark passenger is out in the open, and we're in the middle of the fight.

But let's not forget that the battle isn't about eradicating the past. It's about accepting it, coming to terms with who we are, and moving forward with our chaotic side in check.

YOU CAN'T "CANCEL" THE BEAST

I've taken you on quite a journey with this chapter. So let's bring it home.

Look around you. We don't have peace, we don't have atonement, we don't have empathy, and we don't have healing. Every time you turn on the news, some cartoon character, author, book, actress, or private citizen is being canceled, discontinued, fired, or destroyed. All in the name of "accountability" or "justice" for an amorphous group or to quiet a small but rowdy online mob.

It's easy to say we just need to rediscover the virtue of

forgiveness. But there's a blockage in our veins that makes even approaching the task of forgiveness a huge hurdle. It's exactly what Yoda had to conquer in *The Clone Wars*: hubris, ego, and self-righteousness.

One of the things I've been most surprised by with millennials and Gen Zers is that for two generations who came of age online with massive digital footprints documenting the stupidity of their youth, they seem incredibly eager to litigate each other's sins in the public square. "Cancel culture" went from being a social media punchline to an issue of immense national concern in just a matter of years. There's a real sense that we're all being watched by one another, and that any day now someone is going to dig deep enough into your social media history to uncover a skeleton. Your life will be put on hold. Your character will be called into question. You may apologize. Either way, you'll be "canceled."

How did we become simultaneously so self-loathing and so arrogant? I think it has something to do with how the social media era has allowed people to curate ideal versions of themselves to present to their peers. We can pick and choose what is seen. We filter our lives through sepia and clarendon filters like you'd find on Instagram. At a certain point, it becomes easy to forget the not-so-great posts we might have made ten years back. We start to believe our own distortions about who we are and forget about our brokenness.

We're in the midst of a hubris pandemic. The widespread mentality of the day is poisonous. If you can hide your sins well enough and whip yourself convincingly in the public square, you're well positioned to be the judge and jury of others on social media or in the pages of the *New York Times* or the *Washington Post*.

It needs to stop.

PEACE AND PURPOSE

We all have things in our lives that help to keep us humble. I value my Christian faith for a lot of reasons, chief among them that it orders my life and gives me purpose, direction, and a sense of hope. But right up there with hope is an almost daily recognition that I'm a work in progress. Star Wars has always done the same thing for me as a fan. It's a story that asks me to look in the mirror and reckon with my brokenness.

Whether in our personal lives or our history books, we'll always struggle with the crushing weight of human mistakes and our shared capacity for evil. Both the failings of our own and those of our forefathers will always haunt us. But recognizing that fact is the beginning of redemption. You have to see your shortcomings, name them, and know them in order to own them. As Yoda says to Luke in *The Last Jedi*, "The greatest teacher, failure is."

When you live your life in the knowledge of your own imperfection and in the hope of redemption, extending forgiveness to others comes easier. And for yourself, it makes finding peace and purpose in life more attainable.

The next time you watch Star Wars and see a character vanish into the ether or become "one with the Force," I want you to remember their debts to mankind didn't vanish along with them. They're still there. The rest of the galaxy has to live and wrestle with the consequences of their mistakes. In an ideal story, your reformed villain doesn't punch out at the very end and skip the part where they try to make amends. But those aren't the Star Wars stories we have, at least not on the big screen.

Instead, I want you to be asking, "Am I really certain that I'm much better than them?"

Maybe you are in this moment. But what about tomorrow?

Tips: Redemption Starts within You—Here's How to Begin That Journey

- **You're a work in progress.** Embrace life being a journey of self-discovery, moral restoration, and change. But bear in mind: you owe it to everyone around you to give them space for their own redemptive journey.

- **Take one step at a time.** In your own search for redemption, you can't take it all on at once. In the time you have available to you, set small goals for improvement and cleaning up the messes you've made.

- **Enter the cave.** Whether it's with Star Wars, at church, in a temple, or synagogue, or in quiet meditation, spend some time with the sides of yourself you're not fond of. What Star Wars teaches us is that our darkness isn't an alien or outside force, but an equal part of our being waiting to be recognized. That doesn't mean you hand it the keys to the car.

- **Say you're sorry.** This is elementary school advice, but there's an increasing need to be reminded of this virtue. If you messed up or said something you didn't mean or made an error in the past, say you are sorry. Then move on. Maybe your persecutors don't move on, but that's on them—not you.

- **Reach out.** When we don't bother to seek redemption in this life it's often because of overwhelming shame or our fear of rejection. Calling up your estranged child or friend to see how they're doing may be scary: what if they don't want to talk to you? Fear is the way to the dark side. Reject it. Choose hope. Redemption is just downstream.

CHAPTER 6

POWERFUL LIGHT, POWERFUL DARK

"You were supposed to bring balance to the Force, not leave it in darkness."

—Obi-Wan Kenobi

BALANCE

HAVE YOU EVER WONDERED why the Jedi in Episodes I, II, and III of Star Wars were so consumed with a prophecy about a "Chosen One" who would bring "balance to the Force"? It's okay to admit the whole thing was somewhat confusing. The stated belief of the Jedi throughout the prequel trilogy was that Anakin Skywalker, discovered by Master Qui-Gon Jinn on a remote desert planet living under slavery, was destined to destroy the Jedi's dark-side rivals, the Sith, and "restore balance to the Force." How convenient.

This raises a key question: why do the Jedi, the galaxy's avatars for the light side of the Force, view the total destruction of the Sith as an act of balance? If light and dark exist on two ends of a scale and one wipes out the other, that would be imbalance. It's not complicated. You see, the Sith had been virtually extinct for a millennium according to the Jedi Council in *Episode I: The*

Phantom Menace (1999). When Qui-Gon arrived on Coruscant with the newly freed Anakin, he told them of his brief lightsaber battle in the desert with a mysterious attacker (Darth Maul). The council wanted an immediate investigation to determine if the Sith were in fact resurgent. To the Jedi, this presented a mortal threat, and while the Sith would ultimately bring about the demise of the Jedi Order by the end of the prequel trilogy, it is quite clear that the Jedi were the architects of their own destruction. In the end, the Jedi Order would be wiped out. Two notable survivors, Obi-Wan Kenobi and Master Yoda, spent the next twenty years in hiding while the newly ascendent Sith ruled the galaxy. In a numeric sense, some semblance of balance was restored, but the thing about the dark side is that it hungers, devours, and grows. Cosmic balance was once again way out of order.

And so began a tug-of-war in the Star Wars universe between the forces of light and dark, democracy and dictatorship, chaos and order that eventually comprises nine trilogy films and a whole host of spin-offs. After approximately one thousand years of democracy, the Galactic Republic collapsed and became the Empire, ushering in a period of Sith rule for twenty-four years. A scrappy band of dissidents known as the Rebel Alliance would undo the Empire, defeating them first during *Return of the Jedi*'s Battle of Endor and more conclusively years later at the Battle of Jakku. It was the Empire's last stand, and the wreckage would serve as a home to Rey, as seen in *Episode VII: The Force Awakens* (2015), when she's making dinner inside the remains of a giant AT-AT walker.

Following the fall of the Empire, the New Republic era was a return to democracy and self-governance in the galaxy. The New Republic managed to last thirty years until a neo-imperial movement known as the First Order wiped out their entire fleet and capital ships with a weapon of mass destruction, kicking off a new period of total war between these dueling tribes of darkness and light. By the end, it turned out that the same Sith lord, Emperor Palpatine, was the puppet master of the entire saga. His eventual defeat at the hands of Rey and his fleet's demise in *Episode IX: The Rise of Skywalker* (2019) ended yet another cycle of political tumult in the galaxy far, far away.

THE DEMOCRACY ROLLER COASTER

As you can tell from this summation, life in the Star Wars universe is a bit of a roller-coaster ride. But it's not too dissimilar from our own experiences with government, where power is always changing hands. Americans, well, we're kinda lucky. We haven't experienced what folks in South America or the Middle East would know as "regime change," but instead just endure a regular changing of the guard in the form of peaceful transfers of power. The certification of Joe Biden's presidential win in 2020 and his subsequent inauguration stands out as a notable exception. Between his win and taking the oath of office, there was a mob attack on the US Congress intended to intimidate members and invalidate the counting of Electoral College ballots.

These have been scary times to live through, no matter where you stand in the great divide.

Four years of Jimmy Carter, eight of Reagan, four for Bush, eight for Clinton, and then another Bush, followed by Obama, Trump, and now Biden. Blue, red, red, blue, red, blue, red, and blue. Talk about whiplash. We go on this ride because we can, and that's something to be thankful for. But we also go on it because voters love sweeping change, but only so long as their taxes remain the same, no jobs are threatened, all social programs remain untouched, and political institutions stay wholly unreformed. You see what I'm getting at here?

We want balance and we want continuity, but we also want vision, energy, and dynamism. We want space to build private lives and communities that adhere to our values, but we don't want our political opposites to feel empowered to build communities to *their* liking. It's a question for the ages: if you believe something is true beyond the shadow of a doubt, shouldn't you then think everyone else ought to also believe it? A progressive Californian can sleep soundly at night knowing that their state allows for the existence of sanctuary cities, shielding undocumented immigrants from legal threat and deportation. But are they willing to tolerate Texas handling illegal immigration in a very different, more stern fashion? Should North Carolina be allowed to have policies requiring work in order to receive state assistance while New York makes welfare as easy as showing up at city hall and signing on the dotted line?

In the end, it seems like no political faction gets what it

wants in the communities in which they live. The prying eye of a national news media, Hollywood celebrities, and, of course, the White House are always standing by to name, shame, or sue their political opponents over state or local laws that are out of step with their own values. Every election becomes monumental in importance, because each side is convinced that they have an obligation to rein in power.

But pursuing such ends could spell disaster, of Death Star proportions, for our own republic. We need balance, and not the kind of balance the Jedi prescribed in their Chosen One prophecy.

BALANCE AS A PRINCIPLE

What does it mean to have balance? It's a subject within nearly every world religion and a consistent theme throughout works of epic fiction. It's dualism; it's yin and yang as depicted in Chinese philosophy; it's Christ being sent to humanity to offer deliverance from original sin. Balance is often talked about as the scale checking systems both of order and of chaos, and to its credit, humanity seems to have a base understanding that too much of one thing, or excess, is a road to ruin.

This very principle is enshrined in the US constitutional order through the principle of checks and balances and the separation of powers. The idea is powerful, albeit simple and still imperfect. You have these executive, legislative, and judicial branches of government, all bestowed with separate powers and varying measures of authority. Each is invested with incentives that would lead them to safeguard their own power and hold the other branches at bay, keeping them from accumulating more. Grafted atop a vision of government in which federal power clashes with state and local power, the American way of government strives for balance, knowing that human nature trends toward excess.

Then you have the Bill of Rights, ten amendments within the US Constitution that serve as a road map for the baseline guarantees of American liberty. It outlines the freedoms any and every American should expect to enjoy, and that government (federal, state, or local) cannot withhold. That's not to say this guarantee has been historically fulfilled. Far, far from it. We didn't see an America that honored the basics of the Bill of Rights until the 1960s. That's also not to say certain politicians today won't try their darndest to abridge those rights—no, they try all the time and, in some cases, succeed in the short term as long as the Supreme Court doesn't get involved. Just ask a New Yorker about how easy it is to own a firearm in accordance with their Second Amendment rights.

Many of the Founders thought a bill of rights would be dangerous, because if you were to write out and affirm what the specific rights of the people were, then in a sense those rights would be limited to only what's listed. So what they did was outline the fundamental rights of Americans in Amendments I–VIII, and they specified what Congress has the authority to do (levy taxes, coin money, make war, etc.). Amendments IX–X are where it gets really interesting.

The Ninth Amendment says, "The enumeration in the Constitution of certain rights shall not be construed to deny or disparage others retained by the people." The Tenth Amendment seems to follow up and expand on that by saying, "The powers not delegated to the United States by the Constitution, nor prohibited by it to the States, are reserved to the States respectively, or the people."

This short collection of words defines the American experiment and for a time, enacted a form of balance. The enumeration of the government's powers and delegation of everything not mentioned to the states (or the people) was a radical balancing measure for its time, and still is today.

WHAT DOES BALANCE MEAN
IN STAR WARS?

I told you already about the Jedi and their catastrophically skewed view of balance, embodied in a "Chosen One" prophecy that they understood to mean the total defeat of their enemies on the dark side. But Star Wars has never really been crystal clear about what the prophecy did in fact mean, or if it was fulfilled by Anakin, or by Luke Skywalker, or by Rey in the latest sequel trilogy. This matter is up for debate among fans, and frankly there's no right answer.

Nevertheless, Star Wars didn't give up on the theme of balance after the prequel trilogy. In the sequel films, starting with *Episode VII: The Force Awakens* (2015), the necessity of balancing the Force is mentioned in the first three minutes. We see a new hero, Poe Dameron, meeting with a mysterious old man in a desert village on the planet of Jakku. The old man, Lor San Tekka, hands over to Dameron and his droid, BB-8, a data drive holding coordinates that may help in the finding of Luke Sky-walker. The now-aged Jedi Master has been lost to the galaxy for many years, and in his absence, darkness has risen again. Balance in the galaxy is being thrown off yet again by the rise of the First Order, a massive military junta aspiring to bring back the supposed glory days of the Empire.

"Without the Jedi, there can be no balance in the Force," says Lor San Tekka to Dameron. But he's wrong, or at least he is so according to the Jedi he seeks to find and presumably deploy as a check against the First Order. Luke Skywalker would eventually be found, and he wants nothing to do with this quasi-religious turf war over the galaxy. "I will never train another generation of Jedi," he says. "I came to this island to die. It's time for the Jedi to end." This broke some fans' hearts.

Luke arrived at this position after an incredible trauma. He undoubtedly saved the galaxy from the darkness of the Sith and their empire when he helped to redeem Darth Vader in *Episode VI: Return of the Jedi* (1983). Vader famously tossed his master, Emperor Palpatine, down a pit within the Death Star only to die himself shortly after. The Sith were defeated. The Jedi had come roaring back and emerged victorious. But this outcome was just a mirror image of what happened to the Jedi in *Episode*

III: Revenge of the Sith (2005). They had destroyed an enemy, tilting the order of the galaxy back in their direction.

Luke went on to rebuild the Jedi Order after defeating the Empire only to have one student, the son of Han and Leia, Ben Solo, fall to darkness and destroy it all. Simply defeating the bad guys does not constitute *balance*. Luke now understood this.

The tug-of-war continues. The more practitioners of the light attempt to fully sideline the dark, the harder the backlash gets. In politics you often hear this effect likened to a clock's pendulum swinging back and forth. Democrats will take power and wield it indiscriminately, and the pundits will say, "Just watch. The pendulum will swing back the other way, eventually." And it does. But if you were to catch the pendulum as it is swinging and hold it on one side long enough, when you let it go, it's going to not just swing to the other side but instead crash through the walls of the clock.

That's life in the Star Wars universe.

It might be useful right now to define what the light side and dark side of the Force even are. At its most simple, the light side is serenity, the promotion of harmony and of logic in place of one's base passions. The light promotes selflessness and the pursuit of knowledge to solve problems. The dark side is raw emotion and indulgence; it is selfishness and the accumulation of power above all else. The dark side calls on its adherents to embrace fear, because reveling in being afraid puts you on the path to finding ways to control or dominate that which makes you anxious. It's important to note that because the dark side hinges on excess, its practitioners are insatiable. Single characters like Palpatine have the potential for creating huge catastrophic imbalances in the Force, and you see that play out across the nine Star Wars trilogy films.

Palpatine is evil. But the light and dark themselves are not synonymous with good and evil. While the dark certainly makes more space for wicked acts to occur with its intense focus on self-gratification, the dispassionate zen of the light can lead to an aloofness that can sometimes accommodate evil.

Take, for example, the Jedi's disinterest in ending slavery on Anakin Skywalker's home world of Tatooine. If their primary virtue as an organization of the light was to keep peace, then the force that would have been required to vanquish the institution of slavery on Tatooine would likely run afoul of that. Qui-Gon Jinn was emphatic about this point in *Episode I: The Phantom Menace* (1999), when he took an interest in Anakin for his unusual strength in the Force: "We didn't come here to free slaves." Well, why not? This nagging moral question is what would keep Anakin up at night for years to come, filling him with a righteous anger that would boil over many years later and manifest itself in the Empire.

WRITING YOURSELF THE ULTIMATE
PERMISSION SLIP

"This is the most important election of our lifetime," is perhaps the most repetitive and aggravating trope in punditry and politics. You've heard it all too often for the past decade or so. Rest assured, the elections of 2022 will be described as the most important midterms *ever*, just like those of 2018.

But I also missed a great many of the "most important elections ever." Apparently, 1980 was pretty significant. Nancy Reagan said as much. So did Truman in 1952. So did Obama in 2008. You can go back as far as 1856, when the *New York Times* said of a Pennsylvania legislature contest, it was "by all parties conceded the most important election that has been held since the organization of our Government."*

Why do pundits and politicians always spout this line off and go unchallenged? I've seen it on political panels for cable news shows on which I've appeared. Someone will say it, and everyone in the room just suddenly begins to nod in unison as if it's a profound insight. At some point it probably was. I'll concede that, in retrospect, the 2000 election seems pretty darn consequential now. No one knew they were electing a would-be wartime president with the September 11, 2001, attacks right around the corner. In fact, a lot of elections feel consequential in hindsight.

Without a doubt, Abraham Lincoln's certainly was. After all, Americans were picking a leader who would steer the nation through four years of civil war and carnage that Americans today could hardly imagine. But to those dosed up on the fervor of partisan politics, we haven't made much progress since 1860.

---

* Jeff Greenfield, "The Least Important Election of Our Lives," August 23, 2020, Politico, https://www.politico.com/news/magazine/2020/08/23/the-least-important-election-of -our-lives-400075.

And when that's your mindset, there's no issue with calling any election you'd like "the most important election of our lifetime." You're doing something you must if you want to make change—you're writing your side a permission slip to do whatever is necessary to win.

It's like what Palpatine told Anakin when he commanded him to go murder all the Jedi at the Jedi Temple in *Revenge of the Sith*: "Do not hesitate—show no mercy." In Palpatine's stated reasoning, if they weren't all destroyed, it would be "civil war without end."

This attitude can help to explain the 2016 essay in the *Claremont Review of Books* by an author writing under the pseudonym Publius Decius Mus, entitled "The Flight 93 Election."* Flight 93, of course, refers to the plane taken back by force by the passengers and crashed into a field in Somerset County, Pennsylvania, on 9/11. The essay functioned as a Republican battle cry in that election year—in the most literal sense.

See for yourself: "2016 is the Flight 93 election: charge the cockpit or you die," reads one of the key passages. "You may die anyway. You—or the leader of your party—may make it into the cockpit and not know how to fly or land the plane. There are no guarantees. Except one: if you don't try, death is certain. To compound the metaphor: a Hillary Clinton presidency is Russian roulette with a semi-auto. With Trump, at least you can spin the cylinder and take your chances."

---

* Publius Decius Mus AKA Michael Anton, "The Flight 93 Election," September 5, 2016, *Claremont Review of Books*, https://claremontreviewofbooks.com/digital /the-flight-93-election/.

Talk about extreme.

We now know the essay's writer to have been Michael Anton, an essayist and political speechwriter who went on to serve in the Trump administration on the National Security Council. Anton's bleak reference to that fateful flight as an analogy for our national situation was shocking to some. But let's take Anton seriously for a moment and question how someone might come to believe this, that partisan politics as usual was no longer a game of slightly varying tax rates and regulatory policy, but instead a life-or-death affair.

If you listen daily to talk radio or read the *New York Times*, this is probably what you're being told. And you know what? Maybe it's correct. The tentacles of the federal government have grown so long and so powerful that they are squeezing out all of the distance that Americans used to feel from the machinations of Washington. Presidents now make war as they please. They enact regulations on industries they dislike with the stroke of a pen, impacting livelihoods nationwide on a whim. The office of the president increasingly sets the agenda for its colleagues in Congress, when it used to be the other way around. The president nominates judges for life tenure to the Supreme Court, whose role in American life has grown more consequential than it was ever intended to be.

In short, the stakes of every election are higher than they should be. Together as a people we have built a Death Star, and we're constantly wrestling with one another for the controls. Our target?

One another.

FLIGHT 93 IN A GALAXY FAR, FAR AWAY

Following the rise of the Empire, Emperor Palpatine had a unique challenge in trying to keep thousands of star systems corralled into one united government. Remember, they had just witnessed years of sectarian conflict in the Clone Wars, and it was that very chaos, with a monumental death toll topped off by allegations of a Jedi coup, that allowed Palpatine to seize total power in the name of restoring order.

You have to imagine there was a bit of a honeymoon period for the Empire. At first, everyone probably loved the idea, thus the "thunderous applause," and then realized a few days or weeks later that their galactic senators had pulled the equivalent of a Las Vegas shotgun wedding performed by an Elvis impersonator. As soon as that warm fuzzy feeling, or total intoxication, wears off...you have a major problem. This is more or less where the Death Star comes into play.

Grand Moff Tarkin, played by the late and great Peter Cushing, fully explains the logic of the Death Star project in the original Star Wars, *Episode IV: A New Hope* (1977), when he posits to the imperial hierarchy that "fear will keep the local systems in line—fear of this battle station." The idea was simple. Make it so that worlds within the Empire couldn't even think about things such as secession or insurrection without the looming threat of total and instant annihilation. If the Senate agreeing to Palpatine's Empire was akin to a Vegas wedding, the Death Star was a blanket ban on getting an annulment.

This was known as the Tarkin Doctrine, which was similar in some ways to the US military doctrine during the Cold War, "mutually assured destruction." The idea was that two nuclear states could maintain an uneasy peace, because failure to do so would mean an exchange of nuclear rockets—and total devastation. In Star Wars, only the Empire had the weapon of mass destruction, but in both scenarios the common denominator was peace through fear.

But did the Death Star end up crippling the galaxy with fear to the point where the Emperor could govern as he pleased? While we know the Rebel Alliance eventually breaks the Empire in *Episode VI: Return of the Jedi* (1983), the answer to this question really lies within *Rogue One: A Star Wars Story* (2016). The Rebellion at this point in the Star Wars tale is fledgling, disorganized, and fractious. There's discontent about the Empire, but very little unity on what to do about it. That's why you have the Rebel Alliance we recognize, led by the white-robed Mon Mothma and Bail Organa, pitted against a more chaotic and violent anti-imperial force named Saw Gerrera. Some in the Alliance think that the democratic process can still save them. If just enough senators were to vote to dismantle Palpatine's authority, surely things could go back to the way they once were?! Others are keenly aware that the growing power of the Empire is a life-or-death-level crisis, and that not launching a full-scale armed rebellion is tantamount to walking oneself to the guillotine.

Remember, the galaxy does not know about the Death Star project at this point. The test conducted in *Rogue One* that wiped out an entire city was explained to the Senate as a "mining disaster." When our reluctant hero Jyn Erso comes to the Rebel Alliance with intel on the Death Star and how to destroy it, many in the room don't even believe her announcement that the Death Star exists.

One rebel posits, "*If* the Empire has this kind of power, what chance do we have?"

Erso responds, "What chance do we have? The question is 'What choice?'"

Jyn Erso was right, and the majority of the wayward Rebellion agreed with her. In that moment, the Rebel Alliance became more than an organization: it blossomed into a widespread movement and cascaded toward revolution. The point here is, of course, that we shouldn't want to create a climate in our own country in which people on either side feel under threat from government in the way Erso and the rebels did here.

THERE'S A SERIOUS DISTURBANCE IN THE FORCE

Unfortunately, that ever-present feeling of existential threat is exactly what is going on here. In the century and a half following a devastating civil war brought on by slavery and decentralized government run amok, American government has reached a point where it is now characterized by the struggle for control over the levers of federal power. Sure, political parties have always been invested in this fight, but now it has consumed everyday people. Americans are fearful about what their political opposites will do to them if and when they win power.

It's become a political arms race when what we need is disarmament.

And the reason for that is actually quite good: it's a part of our national success story. The United States does not look the same as it did a century ago. What used to be a country with a very clear white, Christian, Eurocentric identity is now an eclectic multiracial nation with room for all sorts of competing value systems and faiths. There are obviously upsides to being more culturally unified through a shared religion, but it's better if religious conformity does not function as a be-all and end-all of our society.

On top of that, the vast majority of American history has been defined by a two-party dynamic in which both the Republican and Democratic Parties clashed on the minutiae of tax rates but tepidly agreed, up until 1964, on the imperative of maintaining the disenfranchisement of African Americans. Since then, we've seen the two parties polarize and come to represent starkly different brands of politics that not only split along policy lines, but also demographic ones.

The period of rapid political polarization since the '60s has been frustrating for most Americans, but it's really somewhat normal when held up against other democracies. We've always talked a big game about our commitments to democracy and pluralism, but only recently have we started to try to live that out. The problem is that our political parties are still trying to gather power and govern like it's 1940.

The old Democratic Party of Franklin D. Roosevelt and Lyndon B. Johnson adhered to the politics of the New Deal era with nearly religious devotion. The idea of a vast centralized government that stitched together fifty states with a common purpose and social fabric was a progressive dream that had its moment in the twentieth century, and it served a purpose. A more unified nation was able to join together and win World War II and to build a national infrastructure and housing that ushered in an economic golden age for (most) Americans. Washington's role in breaking up the entrenched racial segregation and totalitarian politics of the South cannot be overstated. But we don't live in that world anymore.

America has undergone several cultural and political revolutions in the years since. Try to imagine your grandparents' shock when Democratic presidential candidate Julián Castro made an appeal in the 2019 presidential primary debates to the imperative that we not forget transgender women's right to "reproductive justice," presumably meaning abortion access—lest you need a clearer example of how fast things have changed.

While our politics have become more polarized and open to participation by all Americans, the ethos of the New Deal era hasn't gone anywhere. Politicians from both sides of the divide talk about their plans and vision for the country as if we feel common purpose, or as if we're all speaking the same language.

We aren't—literally. The Center for Immigration Studies has pointed out that, as of 2018, 67.3 million people in the United States speak a foreign language first and foremost within their home.* Across the nine most racially diverse states, that's one in four people who aren't even actively speaking English. A 192 percent increase from 1980.

I'm not here to make a case for or against immigration, but instead to point to things as they are and look at the choices we need to make as a result. You could cut off the flow of immigration, both legal and illegal, tomorrow and it would not change the larger cultural forces making life in the Carolinas, Tennessee, and Kentucky entirely dissimilar from that of New York, Maine, California, and Connecticut.

We have a glaring problem in our politics today, a disturbance in the Force if you will. And it's not the wave of social change I just laid out here. It's that despite being a nation founded on the idea of mutual cooperation, compromise, and deference, there's not an awful lot of it going around. Instead, we have drifted toward a politics of contempt, coercion, and fear. With the country changing at a pace that cannot be stopped, but not quite at a pace to make America's center-right disposition irrelevant, both factions are either hustling to change the rules of politics or to call on the referees at every turn.

---

* Karen Zeigler and Steven A. Camarota, "67.3 Million in the United States Spoke a Foreign Language at Home in 2018," Center for Immigration Studies, October 29, 2019, https://cis.org/Report/673-Million-United-States-Spoke-Foreign-Language-Home-2018.

EVERYONE LOVES THE JEDI,
UNTIL THEY DON'T

In the Star Wars prequels, a similar governance problem arose because of the sheer size of the Galactic Republic. Incorporating thousands of star systems and not equipped with a military (prior to the Clone Wars) to enforce the law or maintain peace, the Jedi Order took on the role of galactic diplomats. They'd be dispatched by the Republic to settle local disputes, broker peace agreements between warring tribes, and, most famously, intervene in trade wars. Over the course of a millennium, this made the Jedi both loved and hated. It was a vulnerability that a certain phantom menace, Palpatine, would exploit to bring about their demise. By the end of the Clone Wars, which Palpatine masterfully engineered, the Jedi had lost virtually all of their public goodwill because of their centrality to the war. Jedi weren't seen as monks or peacekeepers; they were partisan actors and guardians of a particular regime. Far from neutral. Once Palpatine was able to frame them for an alleged coup, there was hardly any public support left to shield the Jedi from this lie.

I mentioned referees, and in my thinking here the role of the Jedi feels disturbingly similar to that of the Supreme Court. Democrats spent the better part of the Trump years casting themselves as guardians of democratic norms and champions of democracy, while their Republican counterparts stood in as closet totalitarians looking to slash and burn every check on President Trump's authority. They did this while simultaneously

drumming up support for the dissolution of the legislative fil-
ibuster, packing the Supreme Court, and, at the fringes, even
advocating the dissolution of the US Senate. But fringe viewpoints never seem to stay fringe for long.

The distribution and wielding of power by the Supreme Court
has become a growing area of public discontent, because politi-
cization of the institution is dangerously high. As with the Jedi's
thousand years of galactic peacekeeping, it's hard to say exactly
where the line was crossed. But just our recent history offers a
few possibilities. While Republicans didn't start the SCOTUS
Wars, they certainly escalated them. The 2016 suppression of
Merrick Garland's nomination to the court by outgoing president Barack Obama was a deft, rational political move, but in
retrospect, it stands out as an act of arson.

Republicans didn't do it for no reason. Conservatives have
had a bone of their own to pick with institutions, including the
Supreme Court for its dictates including *Roe v. Wade*, which fully
legalized the practice of abortion, and then there was *Obergefell
v. Hodges*, requiring the state recognition of same-sex marriages
nationwide. It's not that either ruling keeps Republicans awake
at night, at least not *Obergefell*, but they're major cultural flash-
points with objectively vague constitutional answers that were
settled by unelected elites in dark robes seated in the glittering
halls of Washington.

National solutions to what many consider to be state matters
have raised the stakes on each consecutive presidency. Eventually, another one of those ancient justices is going to become one

with the Force, and in the eyes of these warring partisans...it's of utmost importance that you have control of the White House and Senate to fill that seat with an aligned culture warrior. Thus the blocking of Merrick Garland, and the smear campaign against Brett Kavanaugh, and the blatant hypocrisy of Republicans rushing through Justice Amy Coney Barrett before the 2020 election. This is war. The goal is not accommodation, or pluralism, or fostering a society where there's space enough for people of all races and creeds—it's domination.

Something has to change. The direction we're trending in doesn't have a happy ending, and if our two political parties are no longer committed to a win-win approach to doing politics, it's up to *we the people* to reset expectations.

The good news is that most Americans believe in the principle of balance in our political system. They want Republicans and Democrats to work together, to find areas of compromise or common cause, and they absolutely do not want to live in a society where their political persuasion is too taboo to be discussed in polite company. While this feels both obvious and true, the bad news is that we certainly don't see this preference for balance playing out in the conduct of our politicians or in the news media.

ATTACHMENT AND IMBALANCE

This chapter has been something of a journey through imbalance within the Star Wars universe and our own, and we've covered a lot of ground. The reason for that is both the remarkable scale of the Star Wars story and the scale of the problems we face today. Balance is the principle of the chapter, but is there a solution here to instituting the balance in our lives that Star Wars offers up?

Yes and no. It's kind of a solution, but it's more of a choice than anything.

Padmé and Anakin were starting to develop "a thing" for one another halfway through *Episode II: Attack of the Clones* (2002). "Are you allowed to love? I thought that was forbidden for a Jedi," Padmé asked him. Anakin smiled. "Attachment is forbidden. Possession is forbidden. Compassion, which I would define as unconditional love...is central to a Jedi's life. So you might say that we are encouraged to love."

Despite Anakin being a living and breathing example of how the lines between love and possessiveness can become blurred, there's an important truth here. Love and compassion are good things. Saint Thomas Aquinas defined love as "willing the good of the other," or to basically assume the best of people. Luke Skywalker saying to Darth Vader (Anakin) in *Return of the Jedi*, "I feel the good in you," while handcuffed in his captivity, is a fine example of this "willing" action. It can be a thing that takes effort. You have to defy other emotions competing for control of your mind and actions, such as fear or anger.

The fall of Anakin Skywalker was, of course, a personal failing, but the rigidity of the Jedi Order and its dogma surrounding romantic relationships sure didn't help. The Jedi's approach was to recognize that romantic love breeds attachment and jealousy, and to keep the whole thing at bay as a result. If a Jedi were to fall in love and want to remain a Jedi, well, they'd have to keep it a secret—not learn to love *better*. The Jedi Order requires its adherents to deprive themselves of emotion in all contexts, while the Sith require you to marinade in emotion at all times. A Sith cannot truly love because their way is that of hedonism, self-gratification, and pleasure. Love, as anyone who has ever been in a happy marriage or relationship knows, requires sacrifice and attention to the needs of another.

THE FORCE WAS BALANCED,
AND WE CAN BE TOO

When Rey finally convinces Luke Skywalker to train her in *Episode XIII: The Last Jedi* (2017), he gives her a memorable lesson on the Force. She is meditating on a cliff and has put herself in touch with the energy of the very island on which they are sitting. "What do you see?" Luke asks.

Rey responds, "The island. Life. Death and decay, that feeds new life. Warmth. Cold. Peace. Violence—balance and energy. A force." At that moment, she was on the path to being part of something special in the Star Wars story.

I would argue that the Force was eventually balanced in *Episode IX: The Rise of Skywalker* (2019) by Kylo Ren and Rey when they join forces to defeat Palpatine once and for all. You have Rey, a descendent of Palpatine and student of the light, joining with Kylo Ren (Ben Solo), a descendant of Anakin

Skywalker and proponent of the dark, to put down the most insatiable and unbalancing figure in the Star Wars saga. What allowed these two equal but opposite forces of nature to unite in this crucial moment?

Compassion. Warmth. Love.

Rey and Kylo didn't see perfection or virtue; they saw pieces of themselves. A brokenness. For them, love was a choice, not an inevitability.

We have a choice to make in our own lives, as citizens, friends, lovers, neighbors, and parents—to love despite. The alternative is what I laid out earlier in this chapter, which is a fight to the death over control. Government either exists to protect our rights or it exists to rule others. I'm a small government guy myself, and that's because I've chosen the former. But to give up on ruling others means I've given up the goal of control and invested my efforts in dismantling the components of government that make it as scary to my fellow citizens and political opposites as the Death Star was to the Rebellion. I choose balance.

What will you choose?

Tips: How to Find or Create
Balance in Your Life

- **Understand the real meaning of tolerance.** Part of being truly tolerant is accepting the existence of people and of things you might find objectionable. Not liking all things. The existence of the objectionable doesn't have to occupy your thoughts and drain your emotional energy. If it doesn't impact you directly, let it go.

- **Identify the troublemakers.** In order to have balance in your life, relationships, or worldview, you have to know what forces exist in your life that are pushing you toward imbalance. In the next chapter, you'll learn more about choice and mindfulness. If your news consumption or social media habits are occupying your thoughts longer than you'd like, you need to take ownership of that problem.

- **"Breathe, just breathe."** One thing I've told my daughter since she was old enough to ask to play with my smartphone on a long drive is this: "You need to be okay sitting for a while with just your thoughts." In order to have balance in your life and in your politics, it's crucial to have a sense of dominion over your own mind. The same forces that call you to play Candy Crush when you're bored will also push you to rush to judgment on news of the day.

- **Sign up for something.** Politics is filling a void in our country created by the dissolution of community ties, whether it be your church, union, civic organization, or an enthusiast club. Having ways to associate with folks unlike ourselves that aren't linked to politics gives us new ways of relating and identifying common ground. Join a club!

CHAPTER 7

TWIN SUNS AND THE OPEN DOOR

"You failed him by thinking his choice
was already made."

—Rey

DO YOU BELIEVE IN FATE? Or do you think of every day as a story yet to be written? Most people I meet tend to be somewhere in the middle on this question. On the one hand, it often seems like the universe and our lives have a natural center of gravity, a trajectory onto which we're born. On the other hand, we all make choices.

One of the most provocative themes in the Star Wars saga is destiny. Qui-Gon Jinn, with his final breaths, insists that Anakin Skywalker is the Chosen One, destined to bring balance to the Force. Darth Vader tells Luke Skywalker that it's his destiny to join forces with him on the dark side and rule the galaxy. Luke later believes Ben Solo is destined for incredible evil, and he goes so far as to nearly murder him in his sleep to prevent it. Rey, in the final chapter of the final trilogy in the Skywalker story, learns she is the blood heir to Emperor Palpatine. With that kind of evil running through her veins, Rey rightly questions if she's the force for good in the galaxy she always thought herself to be, or something malevolent.

So much of Star Wars is bound up in lineage and the mantle its characters bear by virtue of their family name. It's a somewhat medieval notion, but it's not unfamiliar, is it?

We have these debates in modern life all the time—about whether or not we're mere products of our upbringings, or anomalies who somehow defied our programming. You've likely been part of the nature-versus-nurture debate at some point in time. Some kid on the other side of the country commits a shooting in a school, and the nation's eyes turn to the parents left living in the rubble and shame. We wonder, was this *their* doing? Or was this something that was always inside their child, just waiting for its day? Was this fate or the tragic conclusion of a string of bad choices?

Then there's the opportunity-versus-equity debate. Does a kid from the DC projects have the same chance to succeed and prosper as a senator's son or daughter living in material comfort and getting a top-dollar, private K–12 education?

These are the definitive social and political questions of the moment, yet they're also completely timeless. It's all part of the discourse over "free will" and whether or not we truly have it. I used to believe that the existence of free will was both uncontroversial and widely accepted, but that turns out not to be the case. In the highest levels of academia, journalism, and media, it's increasingly in vogue to talk about free will as an illusion.

A fairy tale, they say, that we tell ourselves and our children to rationalize human action and give us all hope. Star Wars, however, has remained unflinching in its commitment to the virtue of self-determination, the existence of free will, and the power of choice.

While there is a case to be made that turning our backs on the notion of free will could yield more lenient and humane systems of justice, education, and overall personal interaction, I'd argue it would do the opposite. Our societal acceptance of free will doctrine, as opposed to what is known in scientific and philosophical circles as "determinism," pushes us to be better people and calls up the better angels of our nature in daily life. Search your feelings: you know it to be true. From Anakin Skywalker and his rejection of the mantle of the Chosen One prophecy, to Luke and his struggle over how to stop Ben Solo's slide toward the dark side, and finally to Rey's ultimate decision to choose the Skywalker name over that of her true lineage—choice, fate, and destiny are always in a delicate dance for primacy in the Star Wars story.

This is a dance that you may recognize in your own life—a seemingly unfettered will in tension with a magnetic pull toward certain people, situations, jobs, or outcomes. But still we make choices, and get thrown off what we thought to be our course in life. I asked my mom once what to do when I'd made a financial mistake and felt paralyzed by the fear that in attempting to fix it, out of worry I'd just make matters worse with another bad call. Her response was simple, and it'll stick with me forever: "Make more choices."

REY FROM NOWHERE

When Star Wars returned to the big screen in 2015 with *Episode VII: The Force Awakens* after nearly ten years of drought, the movie's ending left us all with burning questions. Why did Ben Solo fall and become Kylo Ren? Why the heck did Han and Leia split up? Where the blazes is Luke?! And who is this "Rey" girl?

We find Rey on a desert planet, much like Tatooine, only she's alone. She has no people. Her memory is spotty, but she knows she's been dumped by her parents on the sandy world of Jakku, and she's certain they'll be back for her. She doesn't even know her family name. She is Rey, "Rey Nobody."

Star Wars fans aren't wired to accept this. The saga has always been a story of family, centered around the Skywalker line in perpetuity. The reveal in *Episode V: The Empire Strikes Back* (1980) that Luke Skywalker is in fact the son of Darth Vader—the "I am your father" moment—has loomed large over Star Wars ever since. We just sort of assume as fans that if someone's lineage is unknown, then we'll discover it soon enough, and it'll probably be a recognizable name. I was on Team "Rey Kenobi." That was *my* favorite fan theory.

Fast-forward to the next film, *Episode VIII: The Last Jedi* (2017). Star Wars' writers seemed really dedicated to shaking up fan expectations about Rey's lineage and what it would mean for her future. Rey stumbles through the film in search of an answer to who she is and why her parents seemingly abandoned her. In a scene meant to echo Luke Skywalker's experience in "the cave" on Dagobah where he saw himself under the mask of Darth Vader, Rey has a vision in which she asks for the Force to reveal her parents to her in a reflection on the wall of the cave. But all she sees is herself, projected into infinity in both directions, sort of like when you hold up a mirror in front of another mirror. What's interesting about this scene is that while the answer to her heritage isn't answered, the endless hall of Reys that she sees raises some questions about the meaning of the vision. Rey looks almost like a domino, lined up and ready to fall in a chain reaction. She snaps her fingers, and in sequence, so do all of the other Reys in front of and behind her.

Rey is her own person, but she's not an island unto herself. She isn't acting completely independent of the choices other people have made that naturally affect her.

"Who am I?" is a funny question. It's this existential query wherein you wonder simultaneously about your past, present, and future all at once. Where do I come from, am I merely an offshoot of two parents whose genes got jumbled together, where am I going? Whether you're religious or an atheist, we all come up with narratives to wrestle with this clash between thinking of ourselves as a randomized biological accident of the universe or something wonderfully and beautifully made for a singular purpose.

Not knowing who her parents are is an open wound in Rey's soul. She needs to know. And in the final act of *The Last Jedi*, Kylo Ren pushes her to say aloud what she already believes in her heart to be true.

"They were nobody," Rey cries.

Kylo nods. "They were filthy junk traders. Sold you off for drinking money—you come from nothing. You're nothing. But not to me."

Just as Darth Vader once extended his hand to his son, Luke Skywalker, in search of an alliance, Kylo asks Rey to join him. As Luke did all those years before her, Rey considers the offer, and then refuses. Later on in her story, she'll be faced with another choice about who she is and what kind of person she wants to be. That ending for Rey's trilogy and the Skywalker saga as we know it is one of the most moving lessons on living that Star Wars has ever told.

INTERGALACTIC DOMINOES

So what is "free will"? It's a centuries-old shorthand for capturing the debate over whether or not every individual person is in full control of their thoughts and actions. This may seem incredibly simple, but it's a massive can of worms. Embedded within the conviction that free will exists are questions of crime and punishment, sexuality, addiction, the subjectivity of right and wrong, and whether or not individual liberty even sets us free at all.

Then there's the concept of fate, which is the grim flip side of destiny. Consider C-3PO remarking about the life of droids: "We seem to be made to suffer. It's our lot in life." Droids wear mechanized restraining bolts to limit their inhibitions. They know they're restrained by the bolt, and most will accept it anyway and carry out their given protocol. This is fatalism—believing you exist on a set path, even a horrific one, and resigning yourself to that outcome because that's just "the way it is." A droid is fated to eventually be shut down one day, decommissioned or scraped, just as any human being is fated to die of old age.

But C-3PO's fate isn't necessarily to translate six million forms of communication for any master who claims him and then die. Within the limits of his fate, this droid can still have a destiny. Perhaps it's to play a pivotal role in the downfall of the Empire by aiding rebel leaders, or to help Rey in her journey by agreeing to have his own memory wiped so that she can complete her mission. No one makes C-3PO do these things.

Destiny is what we make of living within the confines of existential restraints, ones you might call fate. The trick is not confusing one for the other.

Determinism, for example, thinks of human action and the happenings of the universe as part of a chain reaction. So— Queen Amidala and her Jedi protectors flee Naboo in *Episode I: The Phantom Menace* (1999), and their ship is struck by a laser bolt in the escape. The ship is hemorrhaging fuel and needs to land for repairs, which leads them to Tatooine and to Anakin Skywalker. From there, things are set in motion and dominos begin to fall that inevitably lead to Darth Vader and the rise of the Empire. Such a view of the story even accounts for randomness in the universe, like when the Sand People on Tatooine just happen to cross paths with Anakin Skywalker's mother, and then kidnap and torture her to death. It's a seemingly random event that pushes Anakin toward the dark side and toward becoming Vader.

Because determinism relies on looking in the rearview mirror to explain history, it's not surprising that it often appears inevitable that things would have unfolded as they did.

CHOOSE YOUR ADVENTURE VERSUS MULTIPLE CHOICE

Free will in the public square is more often boiled down to our innate ability to choose one thing over another, and do so free of worldly or divine interference. We choose to order pizza over pasta at a restaurant; we choose to watch *Episode VI: Return of the Jedi* (1983) and not *Episode II: Attack of the Clones* (2002) on movie night; we choose to speak with cruelty toward a friend who hurt us, instead of speaking with grace and patience.

When I was a kid, I had the Choose Your Own Adventure Star Wars books. These were fun short reads in which you'd get to a scene and be offered three or four choices for what could happen next. Maybe you choose in the *Empire Strikes Back* book to have Lando not betray Han Solo and never sell him out to Darth Vader and Boba Fett. The story would then take a detour, but in the end, Han would likely still end up encased in carbonite and hanging on the wall of Jabba's palace. One way or another.

So I had a choice as the reader, to choose what happened next in the adventure, albeit a choice limited to only three options: A, B, and C. If I wanted none of these, too bad. And that's one way you could capture what the free will debate is really about. Are we the authors of our thoughts and the story that is our lives, or are we just the reader? "Choose your own adventure" is a nice tagline, but it's not all that adventurous when you realize just how confined the range of outcomes really are.

You may be thinking, Okay, sure, outcomes are sometimes limited in nature, but don't we pick freely among options A, B, and C? This experience of having choice is a foundation for why most people, including myself, tend to believe in free will. We'll come back to this.

CHOICES AND CHAINS

Have you ever noticed how humanity has a funny way of always rebranding bondage to be synonymous with freedom? My daughter reminded me of this the same week I was working on this chapter, when she started randomly sharing what she'd learned in class about sharecropping during the Reconstruction era, after the Civil War ended and slavery was abolished. This was a huge trend at the time. Poor farmers, both Black and white, would enter into land rental agreements with wealthier landowners, and they'd pay the rent by sharing portions of their crop. Well, that obviously didn't go well for a lot of sharecroppers. Farming is anything but a stable business. (Just ask Uncle Owen and Aunt Beru, Luke Skywalker's moisture-farming family on Tatooine.) One bad season or extended drought and sharecroppers would find themselves buried in debt, working it off for years to come in service of men who very likely once owned slaves. So much for freedom.

It hit me over the head, thinking about this subject matter and freedom juxtaposed against limited choice. When I went out later for a coffee, I looked in my wallet and pulled out my Chase Freedom Unlimited credit card. This thing had been a thorn in my side for a few years after I'd gotten it. I finally had good credit, and with good credit came a higher credit limit, and with that came, well, buying things. It's not pretty when you then get behind on those payments and the interest rate kicks in. What credit cards sell in many cases is "freedom," or a wider range of possibilities for whomever wields it. You could fly to France and stay in the best hotel in Paris, and you could do it right now.

So you do it. Because that feels like freedom. But then the rest of the year after that vacation is in the past, all your mundane daily decisions will be made against the backdrop of the debt and monthly payments. The looming specter of interest accumulating on your credit card grows larger. Should you work extra hours at your job or take on an additional client even though you have barely any time left for family or pleasure?

Your best friend gets engaged, and suddenly you're asked to be a bridesmaid or groomsman, with all the fun unexpected costs that come with that. Sure, you have the power to say yes or to decline that request, but do you really have free will in the sense that your choice isn't being meddled with by external forces? I'm not so sure.

Your current existence is bound by the limits of previous choices, and, in some cases, the choices of the people who came long before you.

THE FORCE SHALL FREE ME

The ancient philosophers Plato and Aristotle once led a discourse on free will after Plato, in his *Republic*, posited that the human condition is to be enslaved to passion, or our base desires.* Think hedonism: you eat, drink, have sex, and assert dominance over others in accordance with passing whims. Wisdom and liberation from these hardwired vices, Plato thought, came from mastery of those invisible forces. Subjugating them, instead of the other way around. It's not at all dissimilar from what you've read in this very book's chapter on redemption, and the concept of conquering "the shadow" in order to tame hubris and ego. (See Chapter 6, "Redemption or a Reckoning.")

At their best, the Jedi Order embodies this kind of stoic, monkish tradition. They view attachments and emotions as forces that invade their members' ability to think clearly, exercise judgment, and make "good choices." So they try to abstain from those sources of distraction. Free will, they might say, is enhanced by limiting your range of choices in life. Refusing to

---

* Terence Irwin, "Who Discovered the Will?" *Philosophical Perspectives* 6 (1992): 453–73.

ever touch a cigarette means that you'll never have to feel that pain of nicotine addiction dragging you outside to smoke during your child's championship basketball game.

The Jedi's rivals, the Sith, essentially believe that our very existence comes with chains built in. We're in spiritual slavery and born into the service of others, whether that be employers, parents, teachers, or, in the case of Anakin Skywalker, an actual slave owner. Setting aside your passion frees you to steer your actions, so as to accumulate power and break whatever "chains" you feel are holding you down in life. If you've never heard either the Jedi Code or the Sith Code, check them out below.

Here's the Jedi Code:

> There is no emotion—there is peace.
>
> There is no ignorance—there is knowledge.
>
> There is no passion—there is serenity.
>
> There is no chaos—there is harmony.
>
> There is no death—there is the Force.

Now check out the Code of the Sith:

> Peace is a lie. There is only Passion.
>
> Through Passion I gain Strength.
>
> Through Strength I gain Power.
>
> Through Power I gain Victory.
>
> Through Victory my chains are Broken.
>
> The Force shall free me.

If you zero in on Plato's commentary on free will, and even that of a doctrinal Sith like Darth Maul or Darth Sidious, the agreement there is that both our environment and our base instincts have incredible power and play a role in what choices we ultimately make. The disagreement is of course whether or not those instincts should be indulged. Our modern world at least partially accepts this as true, that instinct can clash with willful action—just look at the justice system for a living example.

This is why we have different classifications of homicide, like first-degree murder, where the killer is said to have premeditated and planned the crime before committing it. This classification of murder carries a heavier penalty than, say, voluntary manslaughter, where the perpetrator can be shown to have been provoked—a "crime of passion." While treated seriously, the sentence for second-degree murder is often not as steep as when it can be proven that the crime has been plotted meticulously. This is a good thing. It's mankind recognizing that we can all get a little hot under the collar sometimes and there should be degrees of punishment for it. Circumstance and literal chemistry can reduce our capacity to make good choices. But in the end, *someone* has to shoulder the responsibility, whether we like that or not.

You could say that Anakin Skywalker, having made the big leap to the dark side in *Episode III: Revenge of the Sith* (2005), when he attacked and maimed Mace Windu, could—if he were facing justice today—be tried for voluntary manslaughter. After he snapped, Anakin fell to his knees, saying, "What have I done?"

"You're fulfilling your destiny, Anakin," says the Sith lord, Palpatine.

Palpatine calls it destiny, and that's an easy jump to make. When you're dealing with errors in judgment made in the whiplash of the chaos of life, there's a perverse peace to be found in the idea that these things were simply unavoidable.

YOU WERE THE CHOSEN ONE

Anakin is supposedly destined to destroy the Sith and bring balance to the Force. He's the Chosen One, but in a fit of passion he chooses to become a Sith, betray the Jedi Order, and squash the light side of the Force wherever it can be found. Christians will often say that God has a plan for each of us, and while we make all sorts of mistakes and deviations from it, there are mystifying ways in which the plan is still eventually realized.

It's never been clear to me if this is how religious people rationalize things not going the way they'd imagined, or if they see the existence of a cosmic plan featuring a set end point—but with dozens of routes by which to get there. Regarding the latter, this is maybe how Star Wars works. Anakin fulfills the prophecy of the Chosen One. Eventually, he really does bring balance to the Force. The prophecy just glossed over the part where he shrouded the galaxy in darkness first.

Throughout his life, Anakin Skywalker feels like he lacks choices. First he's a slave; then he's a Jedi, suffocated by dogmatic rules; then he lives out the rest of his life in an iron maiden of sorts, a metallic torture chamber of his own making. If you don't know what an iron maiden is, Google Search that one with caution.

I've noted throughout this book that it's only when Darth Vader is able to visualize a future free of the Sith and Palpatine that he feels serious conflict within himself about his allegiance to the dark. Hope, redemption, and free will are all intimately connected, feeding into one another. When we can perceive our available options—the range of choices we could make, plus the outcomes associated with them—our capacity for good choices grows.

THE BETTER ANGELS OF OUR NATURE

In 2002 Jonathan W. Schooler and Kathleen D. Vohs conducted a study to see how people behaved based on the resoluteness of their belief in free will.* They sorted participants into two groups, those more primed to believe in free will, that they alone were in charge of their actions, and those more inclined toward determinism, the idea that their individual choices were simply the product of environmental factors, biology, and neurology.

What Schooler and Vohs found was pretty shocking. The groups were put in situations where they could feasibly lie, cheat, and steal without consequence. Those situations included math tests and financial transactions. The "determinist" group

---

* Kathleen D. Vohs and Jonathan W. Schooler, "The Value of Believing in Free Will: Encouraging a Belief in Determinism Increases Cheating," Association for Psychological Science, 2008, http://web.missouri.edu/~segerti/capstone/VohsSchooler.pdf.

behaved dishonorably, while the free will group self-policed their actions. They made better, more ethical choices.

Similar studies have shown the same thing. Roy Baumeister of Florida State University looked at students and found that determinists were less likely to volunteer, give to charity, or help others when they were in need of tutoring or other kinds of assistance.* Stress and unhappiness ran rampant through this cohort. The free will cohort, on the other hand, had less stress, more happiness, and stable relationships.

Making choices every day is stressful. I really don't like having to collect quotes from various plumbers and then make a decision to hire the one that I distrust the least. But that's nowhere near as stressful as having no options as all, like having only one plumber in town who can fix pipes. In that scenario, the plumber is naturally empowered to charge you whatever he'd like for either outstanding or poor work, because he is the keeper of the knowledge and there's no competition.

Behavioral studies like the ones conducted by Schooler and Vohs and by Baumeister should always be taken with a grain of salt. Nevertheless, they are important because whether or not there is a God, or Force, with a supreme plan for the universe, or whether or not the Chosen One prophecy is imaginary, these studies were able to show that people may make worse decisions when they can pass the buck and shirk responsibility.

---

* Roy Baumeister, "Free Will in Scientific Psychology," *Perspectives on Psychological Science* 3, no. 1 (January 2008): 14–19, https://www.jstor.org/stable/40212223.

Sorry, Master Kenobi, I didn't want to kill all those younglings—the dark side made me do it.

THE DEVIL MADE ME DO IT

We all make choices. This is what I say to my kid every time she does something ill advised, like piling candy atop cake atop sugary drinks at another kid's birthday party. That stomachache was definitely a choice. She likes to turn this around on me every time I eat all the French bread in the basket at a restaurant and then complain later about feeling bloated.

It's a lighthearted example, but something more serious lies just beneath the surface here. Who knows better? A child—keeping in mind that in children the frontal lobe of the brain, where decisions and reason are processed, is still only half-developed? Or me, the fully grown man with supposedly more psychological capacity for cost-benefit thinking, but who arguably has an intense addiction to bread? I'm not kidding! Bread churns out the insulin chemical in the body, this hormone then wigs out our relationship to the sensation of hunger, and before you know it, your mind doesn't process the stomach "being full" the way it normally might.

Gluttony is considered one of those pesky seven deadly sins, and I hate to say it, but I'm guilty. I'm still as thin as a twig, a natural effect of a lightning-fast metabolism, but that really just helps me rationalize why my bread habit isn't a big deal. But even if my metabolism hit a brick wall and I started blowing up like a balloon, I'd still have trouble stopping before I hit the bottom of the basket.

Are we a hostage to electrical and chemical stimuli happening in our brains? Or are we really "in full control" of our every action in life? I'm sure you know where this is going, and it's a lot more consequential than fluffy issues like gorging on baguettes.

THE BOY WHO STARTED HEARING VOICES

Before Kylo Ren, there was a boy named Ben Solo. The son of politician and rebel leader Leia (Skywalker) Organa and flyboy Han Solo, Ben doesn't have a well-tended childhood. Mom is rebuilding the galactic government after the fall of the Empire, and Dad is off racing speeders and getting into trouble with Chewbacca. At some point in his alienated youth, Ben starts to hear voices. The demons of the Skywalker family history haunt him. The prestige that comes with being Leia's son and Luke's pupil burden him. He's crushed between two legacies.

When you're young, you search for meaning and identity. A lot of us go through phases as teenagers when we look for those things in all the wrong places. Don't get me started on my goth phase. Anyway—Ben Solo goes looking more and more for an understanding of who he is by steeping himself in the mythology surrounding Grandpa Vader and the Empire. Before long he's romanticized it and begun to think of himself less as the heir of two of the galaxy's greatest heroes, Han and Leia, but instead as the next of kin to Darth Vader. There's incredible power in that, and the darkness fascinates him.

By the end of the final Star Wars trilogy, we learn that Emperor Palpatine had been creeping inside the mind of Ben Solo the entire time, whispering to him across time and space in the voice of Vader, manipulating him and pushing him toward his darkest inclinations. When Luke Skywalker first senses his young Jedi student Ben Solo drifting toward darkness, he doesn't fully grasp what's happening. He only knows that Ben has been dabbling with the dark side and growing close to a shadowy mentor known as Snoke. Luke is rightfully worried.

So while Ben sleeps, Luke creeps inside his room, reaches out in the Force to read Ben's heart and mind to get a sense of his future, and all Luke sees is pure evil in the boy's future. Death. Suffering. Murder. So Luke gives up his nephew as a lost cause. That's surprising, considering Luke's own father was a Sith lord who returned to the light after decades of darkness. Remember: Luke's the one who extends grace to Vader. That he can't do that for his nephew in this moment must mean the thoughts swarming in Ben's mind are truly horrific. Even Ben's father, Han Solo, later says of Ben, "There's too much Vader in him."

Luke draws his lightsaber with the intention of killing Ben in his sleep. But he relents. The Luke that we know from *Episode VI: Return of the Jedi* (1983), the extender of grace, Vader's redeemer . . . shows up.

Too bad that in this moment, the Luke Skywalker we know and love arrives too late.

Ben wakes up and witnesses Luke, the hero of the galaxy, standing over him with a weapon drawn. So he defends himself. After that, Ben Solo embraces the dark side of his heritage, and like his grandfather before him, murders his fellow Jedi students.

Is this destiny or fate? Is it what you might call a "self-fulfilling prophecy"? When this full account of what happened between Ben Solo and Luke Skywalker is revealed to Rey, she says to him, "You failed him by thinking his choice was already made."

Indeed. If Ben Solo was conflicted, then Luke's dramatic rush to judgment certainly helped him make up his mind.

ALWAYS IN MOTION, THE FUTURE IS

If it weren't so painfully relatable, you'd be surprised that in Luke's confrontation with the sleeping Ben Solo, he's really just repeating his same failure from *The Empire Strikes Back*, when he was just learning the ways of the Force and experienced a vision of his friends suffering at the hands of Darth Vader. Through the Force, Luke saw a glimpse into a dark future, and then set out against the pleading of Obi-Wan Kenobi and Yoda to try to stop it from happening.

We don't know exactly what Luke saw, but it's safe to say it wasn't far off from what actually was already in motion. Han and Leia were about to be betrayed and handed over to Darth Vader. Han would be tortured and frozen in carbonite, and Leia and Chewbacca would both suffer by watching it all happen. Luke couldn't have stopped this, but he most definitely worsened matters and lost a hand by trying to seize control of a runaway train.

This is where Star Wars seems to tell us, yet again, that we have the power to choose what happens next in our stories, but the range of options we're able to perceive is dependent on a mixture of randomness and our capacity for patience. In the heat of the moment, choices can appear more limited than they really are.

THE DARK SIDE OF DETERMINISM

The philosopher and neuroscientist Sam Harris is one of the most well-known people to publicly favor scrapping our societal belief in free will.* His work on the issue is impressive, and much of it makes perfect sense. He contends that we aren't the author of our thoughts, and that on any average day we are bombarded by ideas and images we didn't choose. We sort through them like a wave of incoming emails, assigning huge amounts of it to the junk inbox and only engaging with a handful of items. This makes sense to me as someone who tries to do mindfulness meditations each morning before work. When you sit alone in stony silence and close your eyes, it's stunning which weird flashes of imagery and thoughts will pop into your head totally uninvited. Part of the routine, though, is to accept their validity,

---

* Sam Harris, "#241: Final Thoughts on Free Will," Making Sense (podcast), March 12, 2021, https://samharris.org/podcasts/241-final-thoughts-on-free-will/.

but not dwell on them. You calmly move them to the junk inbox and wait for whatever pops up next, and then repeat.

One thing Harris argues that doesn't make much sense to me is that if we dispensed with the idea of free will and embraced determinism en masse, then we'd be able to cultivate a stronger culture of grace, patience, and maybe even justice. Why? Because hatred for one another in this construct would be irrational. How could you despise someone who is merely a falling domino in a larger chain of events outside of their control?

That human beings are rational by nature is a quaint idea. The truth is, we're simply gifted with the capacity for reason. We do things that make no sense all the time.

Remember the clone troopers in the Star Wars prequels? They were literally programmed by microchips to eventually turn on the Jedi Order when given what was known as Order 66. These clones, most all of which were stripped of their free will, massacred their Jedi friends and comrades at the drop of a hat. A very small number of them were able to resist or avoid Order 66 by removing their microchips before it happened. Do you think a Jedi survivor, if they came across a clone in the years after the event, would be overwhelmed by feelings of grace and understanding? We see this very thing happen in the animated series *Star Wars Rebels*, when Order 66 survivor Kanan Jarrus, a Jedi knight, meets a band of clones living off the grid in hiding from the Empire they were created to serve. Kanan almost kills them, but his friends stop him. Clones, he feels, lack free will by design, and therefore can't be trusted. Not even the ones that demonstrate they have removed their microchips.

How would you feel if you were Kanan at that moment? I'd have drawn my lightsaber, too, because risk avoidance and self-preservation are more in keeping with human nature than reason or logic.

TO A DARK PLACE THIS LINE OF THOUGHT WILL CARRY US

Imagine if in our own world, in the red-hot political climate we're in, we started to think of our political opponents as being programmed one way or another, instead of as free agents who can be persuaded and make decisions accordingly. Democracy itself hinges on the idea that people are movable and make choices. When you've given up on that, all that's left is suppressing or removing your opposition from the equation.

We're not that far removed from a time in American history when pseudoscientific theory ran amok at the highest levels of society, advancing absurd notions about how variations in skull shapes between whites and Native Americans demonstrated the mental limitations of the latter. This idea is known as "phrenology" and came from early nineteenth-century German physiologist Franz Joseph Gall. His work was used to justify the dehumanization and extermination of Native Americans and was recycled throughout the twentieth century to further other racist, white supremacist ideologies around the world. Who is to say we've really moved beyond this?

It's not a leap to wonder if pairing the philosophy of determinism with advancing technologies like PET brain scans will open up public debate about whether our ability to predict certain mental inclinations, like that of pedophilia or just violence, necessitates action to prevent crimes before they happen. If the human condition is indeed tilted toward self-preservation and risk avoidance, it's exactly this kind of knowledge that could push us toward grievous violations of human rights.

And yet some of the neurological science and work on determinism has incredible value in helping us understand why some people do such bad things. Some people are like Ben Solo. They hear voices in their heads, confusing them and nudging them toward the dark side.

Back in 1966, one Charles Whitman killed his own wife and mother and then climbed a tower at the University of Texas to open fire on students, killing fourteen. When authorities found his suicide note, Whitman described no longer recognizing his own thoughts and urges. He asked for an autopsy to be done after his death to find out if something had changed inside of his brain. Indeed there was a change. A glioblastoma was discovered, a type of brain tumor, that was putting immense pressure on the parts of his brain that regulate emotion. Whitman is just one of many criminals who have been discovered to have developed neurological abnormalities, tumors, or conditions and done horrible things they profess being disgusted by. We don't choose our souls. We don't choose chemical chaos in our brains or the sorts of activity that we understand to be bipolar disorder, schizophrenia, depression, or anxiety.

This is where science is productive. Knowing about genetic predisposition is good. In order to more fully understand an individual it's absolutely helpful to know if dementia or bipolar disorder runs in their family. It allows you to look out for, mitigate, and plan for it. But it can also be traumatizing for a person to realize they've inherited a legacy that could limit their choices in life. It warps your perception of who you are and who you could become.

Let's ground this in something more practical, like education.

FORCE PRIVILEGE AND THE OPEN DOOR

In early 2021 the state of California announced a proposed revision to its K–12 public education curriculum for math. The stated goal of the overhaul would be to enhance "equity" among young students by eliminating the track toward advanced math offerings. Under this system, if you have an extraordinary spark for mathematics, you'll stay in the same class with kids who are struggling to pick up on those same concepts until at least the ninth grade.

"All students deserve powerful mathematics; we reject the idea of natural gifts and talents," says one bullet point in the plan.*

---

* Robby Soave, "In the Name of Equity, California Will Discourage Students Who Are Gifted at Math," Reason (website), May 4, 2021, https://reason.com/2021/05/04/california-math-framework-woke-equity-calculus/.

Interesting choice of words. This proposal provoked a huge reaction from parents and commentators alike, and I understand why. My own kid happens to be taking the advanced math classes at her elementary school in Virginia. She's like Anakin Skywalker walking into his first session at the Jedi Temple and levitating rocks on day one. I don't know where she got that, because when it comes to math, I'm more like Jar Jar Binks if he were to be trained in the ways of the Force—just a disaster. I was nowhere near taking advanced classes when I was her age, and I struggled immensely with math all the way through high school. Naturally gifted—I was not.

By the sixth grade, I'd also internalized the "I'm bad at math" narrative, and it sticks with me to this day. I don't want to shift the blame for my struggles with algebra and geometry, but thinking back to high school I can't help but scowl at how math classes were organized and taught. All of the whiz kids were moved out to the higher-tier math class, and I was kept in perpetuity among students who all wrestled with and had internalized a contempt for mathematics. In this light, I somewhat understand the intention behind the proposal.

The California Department of Education seems to believe that students of color and kids from poorer families are oppressed by the existence of advanced math offerings. This is an incredibly wrongheaded, demoralizing, and paternalistic suggestion. Imagine being one of those kids from a marginalized background and having the educators approach you with the assumption you're struggling because of who you are and where you're from. On the flip side, put yourself in the shoes of a well-to-do kid with wealthy and powerful parents, and you really stink at math. The school system is not so subtly saying that you should be better at it because of your privilege. The shame being generated and fired in both directions here is pretty stunning.

In Star Wars, there are powerful threads within the story related to natural talent and how it can burden or benefit key characters. Ben Solo, while he trained under Luke Skywalker in the years leading up to *Episode VII: The Force Awakens* (2015), was mostly burdened by his innate talents. As with Anakin, Ben's natural talent made him arrogant, but it also caused people to be more harsh with him when he fell short or made mistakes. The expectations game was everything.

When Star Wars first introduced the concept of midi-chlorians, a microscopic life-form that resides inside blood cells and that can measure your Force sensitivity, it caused a huge controversy among fans. The concept is revealed by Qui-Gon Jinn in *Episode I: The Phantom Menace* (1999), when Jinn measures the Force sensitivity of a young Anakin Skywalker. Jinn is flabbergasted at the readings the blood sample produces. For a certain generation of fans, this was a gut punch from George Lucas. It took something strictly spiritual, the Force, and blended it with science and genetic predisposition. Equality under the Force was somewhat demolished.

Decades later, this is still being hashed out within Star Wars and by fans. A 2020 Star Wars comic on the fall of Ben Solo depicts Luke Skywalker working with his nephew Ben and another young student named Voe. Ben is wildly talented, privileged just by the nature of his family genes. He can levitate items through the Force with minimal effort. Voe asks why Ben is so much more powerful than she is.

Luke Skywalker says to her, "The Force can be a trickle, a stream, a river, a flood...for anyone who can sense it. Think of yourself as a door. The wider you open, the more easily the Force flows through you. Some people just start out with their door a bit more open. But any door can open wide."

Natural talent exists. Privilege does as well. But there's also a wealth of evidence that shows that your thoughts and attitude can elevate or dampen both talent and potential. Our ability to grow over time and realize potential is closely connected to our perception of what's possible.

The door exists for us all. But our choices and capacity to practice openness will ultimately determine how open that door can be. All of that is to say that there's a great deal of upheaval happening in public education that's like the kind playing out in California. Maybe your school district is considering similar changes. When I think about how to push us toward a society with more opportunity for all, I wonder if it might make sense to cut down on advanced tracks for different subjects at an early age. Taking the Ben Solos and Anakin Skywalkers of the world out of classes where they are alongside students who are struggling to keep up strikes me as counterproductive.

In the end, what matters more than creating fast or slow lanes for math students is whether or not our systems allow for the choice to opt out and zero in on your talents and passions. We need more flexibility in education and learning, not tight control and the limiting of choice. Remember what got us here. Our ability to exercise free will is supported by the availability of things we can actually choose from.

Just as students can feel either empowered or trapped by their legacy and inherited strengths or weaknesses, so, too, can we all. Here, "Rey Nobody's" experience with family legacy and choice is illuminating. After accepting that she may never know her family or where she came from, Rey and Star Wars fans everywhere got a bit of a curveball in *Episode IX: The Rise of Skywalker* (2019). Rey learns that she's a Palpatine.

REY SKYWALKER

I just about threw my shoe at the movie theater screen on December 19, 2019, when I was watching the opening night premiere of *The Rise of Skywalker*. It needs to be said that there is no such thing as a unified Star Wars fandom that agrees on everything in the canon. I grew up in the prequel era, when originalist Star Wars fans pilloried Episodes I, II, and III and teased young fans like myself for having the audacity to enjoy them. So I'm pretty sensitive to that ugly tradition. That being said, I was not thrilled when Star Wars pivoted backward from "Rey Nobody," a central character development point of *Episode VIII: The Last*

Jedi (2017), to Rey learning she is in fact the granddaughter of the evil Emperor Palpatine.

Long story short, the great Sith lord Sheev Palpatine had been toying with the Empire's cloning technology as a way to create physical hosts for his consciousness to be transferred in the event of his untimely death. One of those early clones was imperfect and didn't possess any Force ability. He was allowed to live free and roam the galaxy. He met a lady, and they had Rey. This part of the Star Wars lore is still a little messy and may get smoothed in future installments. Only time will tell.

But for now, no, Emperor Palpatine didn't have a girlfriend. That'd be gross.

When Rey learns of her heritage, her world is shattered, her sense of self totally demolished. Up to this point, Rey hasn't known how she fits into the grand narrative of the galaxy. She knows the Skywalkers are legends, but she also knows that no matter how much she looks up to Luke and Leia, she's not a part of that larger-than-life family. She's just an admirer. But now, it's worse. Rey is implicated in a legacy of evil, and burdened with a feeling that she's somehow fated to continue the family business.

That's so wrong, isn't it? Parentage plays a role in shaping us, but so does environment and lived experience. Genetics are just the starting point for the story.

In the end, Rey rejects the call to darkness, as Luke Skywalker did before her. She fights alongside Ben Solo to defeat

Emperor Palpatine once and for all. In the finale of the film, Rey is asked by a lowly drifter, "Who are you?"

To which she responds, "I'm Rey."

"Rey who?"

"Rey Skywalker."

This is what I'd call a "making lemonade out of lemons" moment for Star Wars lore. As much as I personally dislike the fact that Rey ended up being a blood relative to Palpatine, it's such an incredible statement for a character to not only reject their family legacy, but also to choose their own family alignment. Taking on the mantle of "Skywalker" is the dream of so many Star Wars fans, both young and old.

Star Wars is clear-eyed about both the existence and the limitations of a free will. There are forces at work in our lives that push and pull us in all manner of directions. Prophecies, birthplace, parentage, and even literal slavery are at work through this sprawling tale. But nevertheless, Star Wars honors a rich philosophical tradition that adheres to the existence of choice in how our stories unfold.

There will always be moments when our menu of options is limited, or when the fork in the road really does present just two ways you could go. There are intellectual avenues you can go down that attempt to explain away even binary choices as being ones where free will is illusory, but they are wrong. We all share one fate: our bodies will grow old, and our hearts will one day stop beating. But that says nothing about what our destinies could be. That says nothing about what you could do with the air you still have in your lungs or the blood in your veins. Believing in a construct in which outcomes are predetermined does not push us to be the best version of ourselves. It does quite the opposite.

We always have a choice. If a choice doesn't take you in a good direction, it's time to make another choice.

Tips: Free Will Is Yours—Here's
How You Can Keep It

- **Find your Obi-Wan.** It can be really hard sometimes to see the choices we have available to us. Our imagination and sense of possibility is somewhat limited to experience. Talk to friends, family, and mentors about the struggles you face and decisions you need to make. We all need an Obi-Wan Kenobi. You might realize by talking to this person that you have more options than you'd thought, and more will to exercise.

- **Consume with care.** Have you ever heard someone say, "You are what you eat"? It can come across as sort of mean in the wrong setting, but it's actually remarkable how well this applies to our thoughts. The way you spend your time, the content you consume, and the people you are surrounded by will inevitably affect the range of thoughts you have to contend with.

- **Quiet your mind.** That doesn't mean thoughts won't bombard you, they will, but learn to see them and then politely place them on the back burner. If a thought is persistent and just won't stop cutting in line for your attention, you may have an unhealthy relationship to the source of that thought.

- **The bigger your world, the bigger the possibilities.** Maybe you don't come from much material wealth or you lack friends in high places, but there's nothing stopping you from trying to be in the right place at the right time. Do volunteer work, take unpaid internships, stay involved in community groups where you can network with unlikely characters from different walks of life. Who you know matters, and choosing to meet new people can create and open doors that were previously nonexistent.

- **It's okay to abstain.** I have an addictive personality. Do you? If you are someone who knows from experience that you have a tendency to slip into repeating behaviors, abstention from risky ones might be in your best interest. You don't need to live like a monk, but if you value being in control, it's okay to not interact with substances or activities that will occupy your thoughts and overstay their welcome.

EPILOGUE

N MY TIME WRITING ABOUT, speaking on, and promoting the universal virtues of the Star Wars franchise, I have taken a fair share of criticism for my idealism as it regards the galaxy far, far away. And I understand why. Star Wars isn't magic or some kind of antibiotic you can take to rid yourself of the infection of political disaffection. It's not guaranteed to save your friendships from decline just by virtue of existing. Swooning over Baby Yoda and talking about the latest installments of *The Mandalorian* series can offer a reprieve from conflict with your loved ones and Twitter followers, but the poison of division, bias, and clickbait will still continue to exist and wedge people apart. So how, then, can the Force "fix" the world as I've contended in this book? I've had to ask myself this, more than a few times, because I, too, have walked in the valley of despair, just like most of you during this time of polarization and pandemic.

I've lost friends, dear ones, to this growing divide. In 2019 my most valued friendship, which I had formed around Star Wars and this very mission of leaning on it to bridge political differences, fell apart. No matter where you stand politically, the Trump years revealed to a lot of us the fragility of certain relationships. The temperature of politics was turned up so high, and the stakes were raised dramatically. I have to believe I wasn't the only one to lose a friendship during that time. It broke my heart. It nearly broke my will to complete the outline for this book.

At a time when I needed to be excitedly sending the book idea to publishers, I felt more like Luke Skywalker in *Episode VIII: The Last Jedi* (2017)—dark, depressed, and defeated. And that wasn't the only thing that nearly stopped all of this in its tracks.

Episode IX: The Rise of Skywalker (2019) was . . . not exactly my favorite Star Wars film. On my birthday in December of 2019, I left the theater in a stony silence alongside my brother, wife, daughter, and father. It was the first time I could recall having been so bothered by the content and direction of a Star Wars film that I had almost nothing to say upon standing up from my seat. It was kind of devastating. In my experience, almost all Star Wars fans have been there at some point or another. I was a kid during the prequel era and distinctly remember getting an earful from plenty of older original trilogy fans about how their childhoods had been "ruined" by the new films. Star Wars fans have always done this, and frankly, they always will. But it hadn't happened to me up until this point.

I won't bore you with my gripes about the film, but will just go so far as to say it's not how I imagined the final film in the Skywalker saga would play out. And this made me sad, and even more doubtful that Star Wars was the obvious force for good that I'd always believed it to be. But like Luke, the hermit Jedi Master on that lonely island—I snapped out of it. And I'll tell you why.

How the Force Can Fix the World is not a manifesto about Star Wars' perfection nor a statement on its monopoly over virtuous themes and stories. And it is certainly not a proclamation of Star Wars' unquestioned ability to keep people united in a world being torn apart by self-interested media and politicians, cashing in on all the bitter division. I think it's okay to be honest and say that Star Wars is caught in the same quicksand as a whole host of other things that were once safely separated from the gravitational pull of the culture wars and partisan politics. This was to be expected. The realm of the political is never satisfied with leaving matters of the heart untouched.

The Last Jedi and the rancorous discourse around it is evidence of this sad fact. The battle lines drawn on social media over the eighth chapter in the Star Wars saga initially mirrored political ones. A vocal contingent of reactionary fans, more conservative in their sensibilities, lashed back against the content of the film. Luke Skywalker's bout of depression and his exile were received as the degradation of a generational hero, done only to elevate a female lead character in his place. A soft critique of animal cruelty in the film and the presence of a purple-haired, pugnacious female admiral who verbally smacked around *The Last Jedi*'s fly-boy protagonist, Poe Dameron, struck a toxic nerve. The fan reaction captured the same energy and rage as the "Gamergate" controversy that had rocked the video game industry a few years earlier. It's a wild story and one you should look into if you want to understand our online versus IRL (in-real-life) politics better.

Predictably, an equally militant cohort of leftist Star Wars fans showed up for the fight. Right-leaning fans leaned on crass YouTube commentary to get the word out about why the film was evidence of social justice warriors having captured the Star Wars universe by way of Disney. Their leftward opposites wielded their institutional power in entertainment publications and fan conventions both large and small to push back and even cast admiration for *The Last Jedi* as a sort of political litmus test. It was an awful time to be a Star Wars fan, and unfortunately it's still going on.

But what I realized while watching all of this go down online and simultaneously toiling over the concept of the book was that Star Wars lives in me. No one can touch it. Another person can't ruin my memories or affect the principles I live by. Principles I credit to my parents, pastors, Scout masters, and, you know... Yoda, Obi-Wan Kenobi, Luke Skywalker, Padmé Amidala, and Qui-Gon Jinn. You can study all the philosophy and religion you wish, but if those readings get dumped from your cargo hold at the first sight of a mean tweet or slanderous article, well, that's on you.

There's this moment toward the end of *Episode VIII: The Last*

Jedi (2017) when Luke has become so angry and full of despair that he rushes to burn down his library of ancient Jedi texts and knowledge. He's become so certain that the ugly state of the galaxy is somehow his fault, and the only way forward is to do his part to erase the past in hopes of properly cleaning the slate for the next generation. The spirit of Master Yoda appears and watches as Luke attempts to do the deed and then relents. When Luke steps away and lowers the flame, the Force ghost of Yoda does the job for him with a bolt of lightning sent from the storm clouds above. The library and the tree that contained it all burns.

Yoda's message to Luke in the moments after is somewhat cryptic, and you could read it a number of ways.

"So it is time—for the Jedi Order to end?" Luke asks. Yoda nods and says, "Time it is, for you to look past a pile of old books." He continues, "Wisdom they held, but that library contained nothing that the girl Rey does not already possess."

Yoda may be saying here that he was aware, unlike Luke, that Rey had already snuck the Jedi texts out of the library underneath Luke's nose. He also might have been saying that the lessons those texts offered were already within her. If the Jedi scriptures were vandalized, torched, or stolen... would they be gone? Would their wisdom be any less poignant and meaningful if the next generation of Jedi were to write rebuttals to those teachings or quibble with the doctrine?

No. They are what they are. They cannot be undone. Can they be challenged? Yes.

For the vast majority of my life I've called myself a conservative.

To me that has always meant that the knowledge and ways of living that came before my time have inherent value. The motivation, therefore, is to defend that knowledge from harebrained revolutionaries who would have us throw out everything that gave us the world we live in today for an imagined and untested vision of the future. Tradition only matters if you share it. Truth is only truth if it's unchanging. New doctrines, new scriptures, and new films cannot destroy what is already safe within.

This is the realization I had that gave me hope during my trials of severed friendships and broken trust. Star Wars, even in its imperfection, has always provided me with the tools I need to face the valleys, so that I can make it to the next mountain peak.

The Force can only fix the world if you let it shape your individual actions first. If Star Wars exists to its fans as nothing more than sacred texts or as a nostalgic itch in need of a good scratch, well...then they're just movies. But if you see Star Wars and the way its characters act, the choices they make, and the destinies they fulfill as being *good*—then stop passing the buck in terms of responsibility for your feelings. They will—and are probably already—betraying you. Pass on what you've learned. Take responsibility. Stand up against the dark, but never at the cost of setting foot into the darkness yourself.

"Once you start down the dark path, forever will it dominate your destiny, consume you it will."

—Master Yoda

ACKNOWLEDGMENTS

STAR WARS HAS ALWAYS INSPIRED ME to look to push forward through challenge, ask questions, live well, and help others. It has also given me community. I owe a Wookiee-size life debt to the people in my life who believe in me and were excited to see this project come together. When you tell people you're going to write a book about why Star Wars is awesome, you can tell by their reaction if they're really *your people*, and I now know who mine are. My wife, Melony, is steadfast in her encouragement and patience with me as a tortured creative type. I have a busy mind and busy feet, and I am grateful for every day she simply smiles and nods as I go about upending otherwise serene days to do work, create things, and rant about projects I'd like to take on. Sylvie, you are my beloved Padawan, and every day as you grow I feel more and more that you're already a full-fledged Jedi knight. I learn so much from you, and you inspire me to think big and not let my doubts and my fears dictate my choices. Thank you for your love and sharing in my passions and, in turn, sharing yours.

Mom, Dad, Michael, Emily, Steve, Andra, Duncan, Nana— thank you for your love and for never making me feel goofy about how much energy I put into the galaxy far, far away. William Walker Smith, you're like a brother to me, and I hope we never have to fight to the death on a fiery lava planet and compete for the high ground to achieve victory. But if we do, I will win.

I mentioned the community I found in Star Wars, and I have to thank the people who made the *Beltway Banthas* podcast a success. That show led straight to this. Thank you, Tirso, Swara, Joe Tavano, and Riley Blanton, for what you chipped into this idea of shamelessly and joyfully blending Star Wars and politics. Thank you, Danielle Adams, Aaron Andrews, David Barnes, Glenn Beck, Paul Best, Stu Burguiere, Misty Callahan, Jared Cantor, Heather Case, Ari Chavez, Mike Cooper, Scott Detrow, Nick Dicolandrea, Andrew Dodson, Ben Domenech, Lea Dulani, Jason Edson, Eric Eilersen, David French, Bridget Gleason, Aaron Gray, Albert Gustafson, James Hallman, Mike Harris, Andrew Heaton, Betsy Hodges, Alexandra Hudson, Carlton Huffman, Brittany Hunter, Van Jones, Tamara Keith, Andrew Kenlon, Lisa Kennedy, Matt Kibbe, Derek Kilmer, Cheston Lee, Chelsea Leo, Isaiah Leslie, John Liang, Jim Lokay, Jon Lovett, Seth Masket, Ben Miller, Gene Park, Alexandra Petri, Clark Reimer, Jason Saine, Kate Sanchez, Andy Seiner, Connie Shih, Mikea Turner, Stephen Wiley, Liz Wolfe, and Bryan Young, and all you other friends, boosters, and Banthas out there who supported the podcast in some way, shape, or form. This book would not exist without you. I want to again thank Glenn, who had me on his national radio program so many times to talk about Star Wars controversies and news, even though I may have rarely told his audience what they wanted to hear. No one has a right to anyone else's platform when it has been built with blood, sweat, and tears—and landing numerous times on air to talk about Star Wars with a guy who has intrigued, infuriated, and enlightened me for over a decade is nothing if not special.

When you come up with an idea for a book, the first thing you might do is shake your head and tuck that thought away. It makes sense for a moment, but then there are times when the idea lingers and begins to take hold of your imagination daily. When that started to happen with *How the Force Can Fix the World*, I went to Kristen Soltis Anderson. Not only was Kristen the first guest with any semblance of a public profile to come on the podcast, but she did so twice before we even had a real audience built. Kristen, your mentorship, humility, and general kindness changed the trajectory of life. Thank you for hearing me out when I had this idea and giving me some direction on how to make it real. Matt K. Lewis, thank you as well for introducing me to the process of shopping around the idea as I looked for a publisher. The advice you gave me went a long way. The book's concept really took shape thanks to the investment of Allan Carey and the Charles Koch Institute's KAP program. I thought I was taking a seasonal fellowship to hone some professional skills, but it turned out to be an interactive career workshop where I worked toward becoming the person I always wanted to be. I'm not there yet, but this project got me a heck of a lot closer.

Allan helped me believe in this project and focus on it. He made some key introductions for me, and those led to a phone call and eventually a sit-down with Leah Spiro, who became my agent for this endeavor. I'd have been lost without her hands-on help with crafting a book proposal and reading and offering feedback on every single chapter I wrote. I'm not a big fan of writing succinctly, and Leah helped me strive for that and see the places in this book where I was writing for an audience of one—me. It's obviously an added bonus that my agent would be named Leah, yes, pronounced just like our favorite space princess and rebel.

Thank you, Sean McGowan, Kate Hartson, Alex Pappas, and everyone past and presently at Center Street Publishing. Taking on a Star Wars–themed book is a unique pick in a very tense moment for American politics. I'm honored to have been given this shot when there are so many other authors with important and timely things to say, vying for such an opportunity. And it would be malpractice to not thank the maker, George Lucas, for daring to challenge the status quo of movies back in 1977 with *Star Wars*. Your spark, your values, and your vision have made so many people's lives unquestionably better. Thank you to all the creatives at Lucasfilm and Disney who are tirelessly carrying the mantle today and furthering the world's love of the galaxy

ACKNOWLEDGMENTS

George Lucas imagined. It's an undertaking I can only imagine to be as thrilling as it is exhausting and even burdensome. The dreams of so many people young and old hinge on what decisions are made at Skywalker Ranch. Thank you for having the courage to step up to the plate and swing.

ABOUT THE AUTHOR

S TEPHEN KENT is the creator of the *Beltway Banthas* Star Wars and politics podcast and host of *Right Now with Stephen Kent*, a libertarian YouTube show on the Rightly network. He is a contributor to the *Washington Examiner* and has been featured in *USA Today*, the *Federalist*, *Vanity Fair*, the *Daily Beast*, *Vox*, and the *Washington Post* for entertainment and political news stories, and has been a guest on Fox Business, *The Glenn Beck Program*, and Al Jazeera English. He lives outside of Washington, DC, with his wife, Melony; his daughter, Sylvie; and his perfect dog, Kylo.